THE STUDY OF

COMPARATIVE GOVERNMENT

THE STUDY OF
COMPARATIVE GOVERNMENT

By ROY C. MACRIDIS

State University of New York
at Buffalo

RANDOM HOUSE
New York

Ninth Printing, September 1966

LIBRARY OF CONGRESS CATALOG CARD NUMBER 55–6675
PRINTED IN THE UNITED STATES OF AMERICA

Editor's Foreword

Professor Macridis's useful and thought-provoking contribution to the Random House Studies in Political Science is the second to explore one of the major foci of political analysis. It is expected that when this "series within a series" is completed, all the branches of political science will have been discussed. These studies in scope and methods are based on two premises: that stimulating and intellectually sound introductions to political science are generally lacking, and also that political science is passing through a period of change and reappraisal. The present study clearly illustrates the various kinds of purposes which it is hoped will be served by the scope and method series: to take stock of what political scientists study, how and why; to indicate what seem to be basic trends in the field; to identify and explain the enduring problems and issues with which students of politics have been concerned; and to give recognized leaders and authorities an opportunity to experiment with new approaches.

Comparative Government—as it is usually called—has been, of course, a thriving subject since Aristotle. This has been due in part to the fact that the comparative method or, better still, comparison is almost inherent in all investigation whether truly scientific or not. But there are other reasons for the subjects studied under the heading of Comparative Government. Often it is the curiosity, keen eye, and wide experience of roving analysts such as De Tocqueville. Certain nations having close historical relationships study each other. Outstanding French and British scholars have taken a great interest in the political institutions of the United States. Occasionally a nation like the Soviet Union becomes so important that analysis and comparison of its political life are stimulated. For centuries, the study of alien cultures has been regarded as an essential attribute of the educated man in Western society. As the tension and rivalry between democratic and nondemocratic forms of government have increased, the comparison of procedures, ideas, and virtues has likewise increased. For these and other reasons, students, scholars, and men of affairs have engaged in numbers of governments and with varying degrees of sophistication.

The first part of Professor Macridis's essay is a hard-hitting survey and evaluation of the main characteristics of comparative government as a traditional and significant phase of the political science curriculum. Without in any way suggesting that this branch of the discipline has contributed nothing to our understanding of politics, the author nonetheless argues that the scope and method of comparative study could profit from a thorough re-examination. It is not necessary to preview his conclusions here. As the reader mulls over the convincing indictment, he might ask himself the following questions: What have been the consequences of a country-by-country approach? Have the methods employed in comparative government texts and courses in any way lessened the value of conclusions drawn? Does the absence of really comparative analytic techniques increase the possibility that cultural bias will distort our views of alien political systems? How have the shortcomings noted affected the attempt to gain reliable knowledge about politics in general regardless of national context?

After characterizing the study of comparative government Professor Macridis then outlines what he conceives to be a more fruitful and systematic approach. As the author himself notes, this is not a full-blown scheme at this stage of its development. However, though the direction adopted is tentative and lacking in detailed elaboration, forward progress is sufficient to permit appraisal. The possible significance of this kind of approach for the eventual improvement of comparative political analysis is worth underlining. Given the needs of political science at the moment, it is important to realize that Professor Macridis raises fundamental issues in such a way that they may be discussed more productively and that his effort is a fruitful one.

One advantage of constructing basic categories along the lines suggested is to facilitate genuine comparison. Instead of treating certain aspects of French, British, Soviet, and American politics separately and in isolation, a single category or concept can be employed to segregate and compare the related aspects of all four systems. The study of comparative government has been handicapped by the fact that surface features of various national systems appear to be so different as to defy comparison. A refined analytic tool built around the concepts of power or decision-making should pave the way for more meaningful comparisons by raising the level of generalization on which comparison is attempted. In view of the growing interest in non-Western or underdeveloped governments and politics, it would seem more desirable than ever to alter the bases of comparative analysis to accomplish two purposes: to make possible accurate and appropriate use of existing political knowledge and to minimize the effects of culture-bound assumptions. A question asked about the ideology of, say, India on the basis of the American ideology or on the basis of what Americans think about the impact of ideas on their own politics might lead the inquirer completely astray. On the other hand, a question asked on the basis of a general concept of the role of ideology in certain general types of political systems might yield usable answers. It might also suggest to an investigator questions which otherwise might not be asked. The construction of a limited number of central categories having wider relevance and applicability is a cause to which the author has dedicated this study. The fact that the particular categories advanced by Professor Macridis are not the only ones which might yield more systematic analysis is to be noted but is hardly crucial.

Probably most of the interest in comparison in all fields of learning lies in the differences which are exposed. Knowledge accumulates from efforts to explain these differences. The search for regularities—for *similarities*—is apparently less inviting. Yet uniformities and their explanation are also essential ingredients of reliable knowledge. Another advantage of the author's approach is that it emphasizes this point and offers leads to the development of techniques for detecting similarities interesting and significant enough to be described and explained. It may well be that the almost exclusive attention to the differences between democracy and dictatorship has obscured what could be learned about politics from assuming that some characteristics are equally typical of both systems.

A third advantage accruing from more systematic comparative analysis is exemplified by the author's use of the term "comparative politics." His rejection of the more familiar "comparative government" is no mere semantic variation. As the reader will readily observe, the suggested scheme is not only focused on formal governmental institutions or political organization. True to one of the dominant trends in contemporary political science, this essay emphasizes informal factors, the dynamic nature of the political process, the role of private groups, and the impact of society and culture on politics.

Professor Macridis comes to the imposing task presented by the present study with solid qualifications. Trained in political theory, an expert on French institutions, and a member of the Social Science Research Council's Committee on Comparative Politics, he has the experience and learning to bring historical perspective and restrained judgment to a new endeavor. He is also familiar with developments in political science which have a close bearing on his specialty. It is easier to criticize than to replace the old with something superior. An exercise in analytical exploration is always risky. Readers will profit greatly from the author's courage.

RICHARD C. SNYDER

Preface

This essay reflects the recent interest in the method and scope of the comparative study of government. Thanks to a grant from the Social Science Research Committee, a consideration of some of the problems of method was made possible by a small group of political scientists and our deliberations appeared in the *American Political Science Review* (September, 1953). Subsequently a conference on the study of comparative politics was held in Princeton, again under the auspices of the Social Science Research Council, which was followed by the establishment of a Social Science Research Council committee on comparative politics (Items, March 1954).

In the first week of April, the International Political Science Association held in Florence, Italy, a conference on problems related to teaching and research in comparative politics and the papers presented have appeared in *Studi Politici* (Florence, Italy, March–May 1954).

Having taken a part in the above activities, I found myself engaged in the reconsideration of the field of comparative politics, and the essay that follows incorporates my own work as well as some of the thoughts and suggestions made at different times by some of my colleagues. Needless to say, however, I am fully responsible for everything I have written and it is with considerable reluctance that I assume such a responsibility. For in the essay that follows I have tried to suggest the difficulties inherent in comparative study rather than attempt to solve them. The scheme of analysis for comparative study that I advance will, I know, be received like all schemes of analysis are, with justified skepticism and with the demand that its utility for comparative study be shown with reference to actual empirical work.

In addition, inconsistencies in the scheme will be pointed out and the comprehensiveness of the scheme will be questioned. My only answer is that I have tried to be suggestive and point to some of the problems we face. It is also possible that logical inconsistencies in the scheme I advance are a reflection of my belief that in a period of experimentation with comparative study, different, even if inconsistent, propositions are preferable to rigid and premature theoretical commitments. In other words, I agree that the value of the scheme lies in its utility for empirical work and since I have not used it for this purpose, it would be presumptuous of me to suggest that it is good. I hope, however, that some may, like myself, find it useful as a tentative point of departure for teaching and future research.

I would like to take this opportunity to express my thanks to the Carnegie Foundation for a grant they made to the Department of Political Science of Northwestern University to reconsider its graduate curriculum. Thanks to this grant the Department made it possible for me to examine some aspects of the study of comparative government and develop new graduate courses.

Evanston, Ill.   Roy C. Macridis

Contents

Contents

The Nature of Comparative Analysis

Students of politics are increasingly aware of the inadequacies of their methodological orientation for the development of a science of politics. There is a persistent demand that, along with both the normative approach to politics and an ethical inquiry into matters of political behavior and organization, it should be the task of the student of politics to search for regularities in political behavior and to devise systems of analysis in the context of which hypotheses can be tested. A distinguished scholar in the field defines political science as the "critical examination of common-sense notions concerning the working of political institutions and procedures."[1] The crucial word is "critical." For if we mean that every generation will have to examine and re-examine the existing common-sense notions and substitute for them a "critical" judgment, then it seems that the development of a "science" of politics is out of the question. If, on the other hand, we mean by "critical" the slow development of verified knowledge on the basis of commonly adopted schemes of analysis, then indeed there is every prospect that the study of politics may become systematic and may reach a generalized theory in the light of which our findings may assume a cumulative character.

Comparative analysis is an integral part of the study of politics. The comparative study of politics suggests immediately the laboratory of a scientist. It provides us with the opportunity to discuss specific phenomena in the light of different historical and social backgrounds. It suggests variables of a rather complex order that can be dissociated from the cultural background and studied comparatively. Political parties, for instance, will differ depending upon the economic development of a given system. Political consensus may be functionally interrelated with political ideology, which in turn can be understood only with reference to the economic and social configuration of the country. More specifically, however, the function of comparative study is to identify uniformities and differences and to explain them. Explanation requires the development of theories in the light of which similarities and differences come, so to speak, to life. They then lose their adventitious character and assume a significance that has a causal, i.e., explanatory, character. Phenomena that have mystified men ever since Herodotus observed the variety of human customs and ways tend to fall into place.

Comparative study has also an important role to play in the more traditional approach to the study of politics in which fact and value are interrelated in the scheme of the investigator. Here the parallel comparison of systems may provide us with important clues about the implementation of values and policies. The need for social legislation, for instance, and its compatibility with political freedom may be studied with reference to political systems which have both, so that the investigation may reveal a clear picture of what such legislation entails and of how it can be related to democratic political institutions. The development of parliamentary institutions and democratic practices in a number of former colonies, when subjected to careful comparative analysis, suggests the conditioning factors that account for the development of such institutions and more particularly for the concrete forms that such a development assumes.

The comparative study of political institutions and systems, therefore, entails the comparison of variables against a background of uniformity, either actual or analytical, for the purpose of discovering causal factors that account for variations. More generally it has a threefold function: (1) to explain such variables in the light of analytical schemes and to develop a body of verified knowledge; (2) to appraise policy measures and to identify problem areas and trends; (3) to reach a stage where prediction of the institutional trends or processes is possible.

This conception of the role of comparative analysis, however, raises the following question: Is not "comparative government" a very old discipline indeed? Political speculation began with a realization of contrasts—contrasts between the political institutions and practices of various Greek city-states and between those of the Greeks and those of the barbarians. Long before it was uttered, the Greeks had discovered the truth of Pascal's aphorism that what is true on one side of the Pyrennean mountains may be false on the other. Aristotle was the first student of comparative politics. His study[2] of the various constitutions of ancient Greece was truly comparative, particularly if we recall that Aristotle defined "constitution" in broad terms: it was the mode of life, which included not only the political institutions of a community but the distribution of wealth, the religious myths, and the education and leisure of its citizens. His approach was also systematic in at least two senses. First, he had a general frame of reference in the light of which he observed his facts—this was his notion that the central phenomenon of politics, or rather the central concept under which political institutions could be studied, was that of citizen participation. Second, Aristotle used the three so-called laws enunciated in the nineteenth century by historians and sociologists—the law of imitation, the law of diffusion, and the law of similar causes—in order to explain uniformities and similarities.

It is equally true that throughout the eighteenth and nineteenth centuries comparison was constantly "in the air." It was called for by the works of the *philosophes*; by the founder of modern sociology, Auguste Comte; by the theories of evolution developed by Lamarck and Darwin and adopted by Walter Bagehot[3] in England and by many others. It was part and parcel of the school of historical jurisprudence founded in Germany by Savigny and was also essential to the philosophic systems of Herder and Hegel, Schiller and others. Rousseauian romanticism had evoked the interest of philosophers in the non-Western societies, while the rapid development of colonialism thrust upon both policy-maker and student of politics new questions that called for investigation. Karl Marx's theories provided a frame of reference for the comparative investigation of political systems in the light of a generalized concept according to which the mode of production in any given system shapes the political and social institutions.

The remarkable thing indeed is that the eighteenth and nineteenth centuries abounded in theories that claimed to be "explanatory" or "problem-solving." They were also based, like all political theories, on certain moral assumptions. Marxist philosophy, for instance, was both scientific in the proper sense of the word, since it postulated a broad frame of reference about human actions in the light of which hypotheses could be evolved and tested, and moral, in the sense that it affirmed a desirable goal. Bagehot in his *Physics and Politics* also postulates a frame of reference and introduces a number of hypotheses in the light of which empirical investigation of institutions could take place, but there was an underlying moral theory of progress in his works. The school of historical jurisprudence formulated a theory of law that was suggestive, to say the least, for hypothetical formulations and empirical study. So were the works of Henry Maine.[4] The hypotheses Maine developed as to the origin of the state, the emergence of individual liberty, and the institutional implementation freedom found in the state, were indeed theories that should have been taken more seriously by political scientists. The curious thing is that they were not. Slowly political science, and particularly the comparative study of politics, shifted to the study of institutions of separate countries; it became descriptive; it shied away from theoretical formulations; it scrutinized the formal external paraphernalia of politics—constitutions, legislatures, administration, decisions of courts and the like. It evaded the issue of what the function of politics was in society. Political theory became moral theory and "political science" became nothing more than an ontology of political forms and institutions.[5]

The comparative study of politics is beginning only now to enter a new stage which reflects in essence the progressive systematic orientation in the study of politics. It is beginning to assume a central role in empirically oriented study. This essay is concerned with some recent developments and problems in this field. In the first part some of the contemporary problems facing the student of comparative politics are considered. The past history and inadequacies of the comparative study of politics are discussed, with particular emphasis upon the lack of systematic orientation, and the need pointed out for a more systematic approach in which some of the old concerns and categories of analysis will have to give place to new. The reader will note that throughout the essay the expression "comparative politics" is used instead of "comparative government," for reasons explained below. The second part of this essay presents a broad scheme of analysis in which the most important categories for the compilation and comparison of data are suggested.

The comparative study of politics is conceived in this volume as the closest approximation to the scientist's laboratory possible for the student of politics. The wealth of material for observation and study is indeed richer than that available to the natural scientist, and the political scientists' limitations have been primarily intellectual. We political scientists have failed to orient our empirical study of comparative politics toward eliciting meaningful and pertinent results; very often we have been overwhelmed by the diversity of facts and have been unable to look for, let alone find, relationships between them. We have not even attempted to establish an orderly way of looking at facts.

Comparative study should, in the writer's opinion, proceed in the following manner: (1) the collection and description of facts on the basis of carefully constructed and generally adhered to classificatory schemes; (2) the discovery and description of uniformities and differences; (3) the formulations of interrelationships between component elements of the political process and other social phenomena in the form of tentative hypotheses; (4) the subsequent verification of such tentative hypotheses by rigorous empirical observation for the purpose of amplifying the original hypotheses and ultimately verifying them; and, finally, (5) the slow cumulative process of "acceptance" of certain basic propositions.

Such a conception of the role and scope of comparative politics, however, may appear overambitious unless it is made clear that it calls for a long and painstaking methodological inquiry. The approach embodied in this paper calls for a reorientation of the role of theory and of the political theorist. Instead of an exclusive emphasis on values in purely speculative and ethical terms or on the study of political ideas in terms of their historical genealogy, the role of theory is conceived as follows:

1. to distill from the body of political philosophy generalizations that can be formulated in terms of over-all propositions;

2. to provide analytic schemes within which political phenomena may be classified;

3. to use the data compiled for the purpose of refining and improving the original hypotheses, and finally for the purpose of developing unifying theories.

It may well be that, given the present state of politics, the development of a unifying theory is premature or even impossible. The development of testable propositions, however, and the elaboration of concepts are not only possible but indispensable. It is only through conceptual schemes that the most significant and relevant categories of politics can be spelled out and studied empirically. It is only through a conceptual scheme that we can tentatively spell out interrelationships between various elements of the social process. Naturally such a scheme need not, at this stage, claim comprehensiveness. But it has to be systematic in the sense that it provides explicitly a coherent, even if tentative, scheme of categorization and points to interrelationships at various levels of abstraction and comprehensiveness. There is hardly any doubt that the theorist has an important role to play here.

To take a familiar illustration, consider the study of Point Four and its impact upon political institutions. What is the field-worker supposed to study? What will he be looking for? How can he measure the political stability or instability brought about by technical aid and industrialization? Will it stimulate the demand for greater satisfaction of wants on the part of recipients and therefore lead to dissatisfaction and political instability? Or can this increased demand be channeled into new institutions and new social classes that will carry on economic reforms without revolutionary political changes? Are all colonial systems receptive to economic aid and industrialization? Here the theorist may draw upon Weber and Marx to formulate for the student of comparative politics the proper frame of reference for the study of institutional development and change.

But the elaboration of comprehensive conceptual schemes is, it has been pointed out, an arduous and long task. Given the state of comparative politics, it may prove to be an overambitious one and delay rather than stimulate comparative study. As a result a number of alternate courses of study—none of which are systematically used at present by students of comparative politics—will be suggested. The problem-oriented approach, and the development of classificatory tables and schemes for comparative study may provide us with more manageable types of research, and here, again, political theory and the theorist have an important role to play. As for "area studies," it is regrettable that political scientists have allowed the anthropologists to pre-empt the definition of an area and define it in such a way as to make it operationally almost useless for political scientists. As with the problem-oriented approach, the task of defining areas in terms of common political traits is a pressing one and cannot be done by the area specialist. It requires a co-operative effort between the theorist, the comparative politics specialist, and possibly the sociologist and the anthropologist.

Another major task for an empirically oriented study of comparative politics is, as has already been suggested, that of data collection and compilation. The collection of data, however, even at the prehypothesizing stage, requires a logical frame. Without it, the collection of data becomes indiscriminate and even confusing. The present descriptive approach in comparative politics fails singularly in the task of data collection because it lacks a scheme and relevant categories.

A less systematic approach for the comparative study of politics is the formulation of a tentative scheme that will take into account the relationships between some of the most significant aspects of the political process with the various nonpolitical, cultural, social, and economical factors. The purpose of such an approach is to suggest *ad hoc* relationships for the study of particular problems and possibly to suggest theories. Although the depth and the scope of comparative study are limited when the particular variables are thus arbitrarily restricted, the conclusions arrived at may provide tentative explanations and eventually pave the way to a more systematic and comprehensive approach.[6]

PART I

A SURVEY OF THE FIELD OF COMPARATIVE GOVERNMENT

CHAPTER ONE

Major Characteristics
of the Traditional Approach

A brief account of the characteristics of the traditional approach and emphasis in the comparative study of government will reveal the source of the current dissatisfaction and will point to the need for reorientation. Comparative study has thus far been comparative in name only. It has been part of what may loosely be called the study of foreign governments, in which the governmental structures and the formal organization of state institutions were treated in a descriptive, historical, or legalistic manner. Primary emphasis has been placed on written documents like constitutions and the legal prescriptions for the allocation of political power. Finally, studies of foreign governments were largely addressed to the Western European democracies or to the political systems of Western Europe, Great Britain, and the Dominions.

It may be worthwhile to discuss briefly each of these characteristics of the traditional approach.

Essentially Noncomparative

The vast majority of publications in the field of comparative government deal either with one country or with parallel descriptions of the institutions of a number of countries. The majority of texts illustrate this approach. The student is led through the constitutional foundations, the organization of political power, and a description of the ways in which such powers are exercised. In each case "problem areas" are discussed with reference to the country's institutional structure. The right of dissolution is often cited to explain political instability in France, and, conversely, political stability in England is discussed with reference to the prerogatives of the Crown, with particular emphasis, of course, on the Prime Minister's power of dis-

solution. The interest of the student is concentrated primarily on an
analysis of the structure of the state, the location of sovereignty, the electoral provisions, and the distribution of the electorate into political parties
whose ideologies and programs are described. This approach will be found
in any standard text and in a number of monographs which aspire to be
more comparative in character.[1]

Essentially Descriptive

It may well be argued that description of the formal political institutions
is vital for the understanding of the political process and that as such it
leads to comparative study. If so, we hardly ever have any comparison between the particular institutions described. A reading, for instance, of one
of the best texts, *Governments of Continental Europe*, edited by James T.
Shotwell, will reveal that as we pass from France to Italy, Switzerland, Germany, and the U.S.S.R. there is no common thread, no criterion of why
these particular countries were selected and no examination of the factors
that account for similarities and differences. The same generally applies to
Frederic Ogg's and Harold Zink's *Modern Foreign Governments*, and to
Fritz M. Marx's *Foreign Governments*. In a somewhat different fashion
John Ranney's and Gwendolen Carter's *Major Foreign Powers* has the
virtue of addressing itself to only four political systems and of discussing
them with reference to some basic problem areas, but again the connecting
link and the criterion of selection are missing. Another pioneer book in
the field, Daniel Witt's *Comparative Political Institutions*, abandons the
country-by-country approach in favor of categories within which comparison is more feasible, but the author is satisfied to include under such
categories as "The Citizen and the Government" and "The Electoral
Process" separate descriptions of the institutions of individual countries,
and fails to make explicit comparisons.

It should be clearly understood here that these remarks are not meant to
reflect on the scholarly quality of the books cited, nor to disparage the descriptive approach. They are meant merely to point out that these books
are limited primarily to political morphology or what might also be called
political anatomy. They describe various political institutions generally
without attempting to compare them; what comparison *is* made is limited
exclusively to the identification of differences between types or systems,
such as federal versus unitary system or parliamentary versus presidential
system or the more elusive differences between democratic and totalitarian
systems.

There are two typical approaches in the descriptive study of political institutions. The first is *historical* and the second is *legalistic*. The historical
approach centers on the study of the origins and growth of certain institutions. We trace the origins of the British parliamentary system to Magna
Carta and study its development through successive historical stages. It is
assumed that parallel historical accounts of the evolution of the French

parliament or the German representative assemblies will indicate similarities and differences. The approach followed is almost identical with that used by the historian. There is no effort to evolve an analytical scheme within which an antecedent factor is related in terms other than chronological to a particular event or development.[2]

The second most prevalent approach is what we might call the legalistic approach. Here the student is exposed primarily to the study of the "powers" of the various branches of government and of their relationships with reference to the existing constitutional and legal prescriptions. This is almost exclusively the study of what can be done or what cannot be done by various governmental agencies with reference to legal and constitutional provisions. Again, this approach, like its historical counterpart with which it often goes hand in hand, describes the political system in a very narrow frame. It does not seek the forces that shape the legal forms, nor does it attempt to establish the causal relationships that account for the variety in constitutional prescriptions from one system to another or from one period to another. A typical illustration of this approach are two recent studies on post-World War II constitutional developments in Western Europe: Arnold Zurcher's *Constitutionalism and Constitutional Trends Since World War II*, and Mirkine Guetzevitch's *Les Constitutions Europeènnes*. To a great extent Ivor Jennings's works on the *British Cabinet* and the *British Parliament* rely on the legalistic approach with particular emphasis on the search for precedents that "explain" the powers of various governmental organs.

The combination of the historical and the legalistic approaches is found in the great majority of books published on foreign systems that purport to be comparative. Despite the fact that they give us a cameralike picture of the development and the relationships of the various political organs in a system, and point to parallel historical development, they do not attempt to devise a general frame of reference in which we can get broad hypotheses about the development and operation of institutions.

Essentially Parochial

The great number of studies on foreign political systems has been addressed to the examination of Western European institutions. Accessibility of the countries studied, relative ease of overcoming language barriers, and the availability of official documents and other source materials, as well as cultural affinities, account for this fact. France, Great Britain, Germany, Switzerland, and to a lesser extent the Scandinavian countries and the British Dominions have been the countries to which writing and research has been directed and which are being included in the various comparative government courses in the greater number of American universities. Again, however, no systematic effort has been made to identify the similarities and the differences among these countries except in purely descriptive terms. No effort has been made to define in analytical terms the categories that constitute an "area" of study. True, most authors seem to identify these countries in terms of a common historical and cultural background and they often pay lip service to some other common traits, such as their advanced economic systems, parliamentary institutions, and democracy. What is meant by "advanced" economic systems, however, and, more specifically, what is the relationship between political institutions and the existing economic system? We often find the statement that Germany did not develop a democratic ideology and parliamentary institutions because capitalism developed "late," but no effort is being made to test the validity of such a generalization comparatively—for, after all, capitalism developed "late" in the United States and in some of the British Dominions. Often statements about the existence of a common ideology are made without attempting to define what is "common" and how ideology is related to political institutions.[3]

There is no doubt that references to social and economic configurations, political ideologies, and institutions that can be found in texts should be interrelated into a system that would make comparative analyses of these Western European countries possible. No such effort, however, with the exception of Carl Friedrich's *Constitutional Government and Democracy*, has been made, and even Professor Friedrich is concerned only with the interplay between ideology and institutions. There is no systematic synthesis of the various "characteristics" or "traits" of different political systems. Yet without such a conceptualization no variables can be identified and compared, and as a result no truly comparative analyses of the Western governmental systems have been made by political scientists.

Some notable exceptions, in addition to Professor Friedrich's and Professor Herman Finer's books, are Michel's book on *Political Parties*[4] and the recent comparative analysis of the structure and the organization of political parties and the relationship between structure and ideology by Professor Maurice Duverger.[5] Another good illustration of a more sophisticated study is a current essay on the French political system by François Goguel[6] in which he points out that political, economic, and social instability in France is due to the uneven development of various regions in the country, thus suggesting a relationship between political stability and uniformity of economic development within a country.

Concentration on Western systems cannot be exclusively attributed to some of the considerations suggested above. An even more important factor was the belief at one time shared by many political scientists that democracy was the "normal" and durable form of government and that it was destined to spread throughout the world. In fact, "comparative study" would embrace more political systems only as they developed democratic institutions. James Bryce put this in a very succinct terms:

> The time seems to have arrived when the actualities of democratic government in its diverse forms, should be investigated, and when the conditions most favorable to its success should receive more attention than students, as distinguished from politicians, have been bestowing upon them.[7]

It was natural that such a point of view should limit comparative study to the democratic systems and that it would call for the study of other systems only for the purpose of identifying democratic institutions and forms. As we shall see, such a preoccupation distorted the analysis and study of non-Western systems by centering upon patterns and institutions that were familiar to the Western observer, such as constitutions and legislatures, but whose relevance to the political processes of non-Western countries was only incidental.

Essentially Static

In general the traditional approach has ignored the dynamic factors that account for growth and change. It has concentrated on what we have called political anatomy. After the evolutionary premises of some of the original works in the nineteenth century were abandoned, students of political institutions apparently lost all interest in the formulation of other theories in the light of which change could be comparatively studied.

The question of sovereignty and its location occupied students of politics for a long time; the study of constitutional structures became a favorite pastime, though no particular effort was made to evaluate the effectiveness of constitutional forms in achieving posited goals or to analyze the conditions underlying the success or failure of constitutionalism. The parallel development of administration was noted, but again its growth was studied with reference to a constitutional setting, as Dicey's work amply illustrates.[8] The growth of political parties was studied, but aside from descriptions of their legal status little consideration was given by political scientists to the radical transformation parties were to bring about in the organization of political power. Henry Maine's and William Lecky's[9] bold hypotheses about the impact on democracy of the development of party government and of the extension of the franchise were abandoned in the light of contrary evidence and were never replaced with new ones. Indeed, Walter Bagehot's[10] analysis of the British Cabinet remained standard until the turn of the century, though the word "party" rarely appears in it, and Dicey's formal statement of the limitations of parliamentary sovereignty were considered for a long time to be the most definitive formulation of the problem.[11] The British people, it was pointed out by Dicey, constituting the "political sovereign" body limited the "legal sovereignty" of the Parliament and such limitation was institutionalized through the courts. Federalism and its development in the various dominions was also discussed with reference to the legal organization of power and to its relationship with the concept of sovereignty. In all cases the studies made were a dissection of the distribution of powers in terms of their legal setting and left out of the picture altogether the problem of change and the study of those factors—political or other—that account for change.

Essentially Monographic

The most important studies of foreign systems, aside from basic texts, have taken the form of monographs that have concentrated on the study of the political institutions of one system or on the discussion of a particular institution in one system. Works such as those by John Marriot, Arthur K. Keith, Joseph Barthelemy, James Bryce, Ivor Jennings, Harold Laski, A. V. Dicey, Frank Goodnow, W. A. Robson, Abbott L. Lowells, Woodrow Wilson,[12] and many others were addressed generally to only one country or to a particular institutional development within one country. The American presidency, the British parliamentary system, the congressional form of government were presented in studies in which the particular institutional forms were placed in the context of the whole tradition and legal system of the country involved. Sometimes such monographs represented great advances over the legalistic approach because they brought into the open nonpolitical factors and institutions or attempted to deal analytically with some of the problems facing the democratic systems. They had a focal point and the description of the institutions was always related to a common theme or was undertaken in the light of a common political problem, such as the relationship between executive and legislature, the growth of administrative law and the institutions of administration, the relationship between national characteristics and political ideology, and the like. The relationships established between political and nonpolitical factors, however, hardly attain a systematic formulation that can be used for comparative study, i.e., for identifying variables and attempting to account for them. Nor is the suggestion ever explicitly made that the particular way in which a problem is studied or certain institutional developments discussed is applicable to parallel phenomena in other countries.

The Problem Approach in the Traditional Literature

A number of studies dealing with problem areas have employed the traditional approach. Examples are studies of the relationship between democracy and economic planning; of representation and the growth of administrative agencies with new economic and social functions; of the decay of bicameralism; or of the efforts of representative assemblies to reconcile the social and economic conflicts arising in democratic societies between the two world wars.

Such studies have usually been confined to the institutional framework of the country involved. Analyses of policy-orientation have not gone beyond the examination of reforms of the formal institutional structure, as in studies of the reorganization of the House of Lords, the development of functional representative assemblies, the establishment of economic federalism, the delegation of legislative powers to the executive, the association of professional groups in policy-making, the integration rather than separation of policy-making organs, and, finally, measures to combat the growth of antidemocratic parties within democratic systems. The study of such problems has paved the way, however, for the abandonment of the traditional formal categories, for these problems cannot be examined in that restricting frame. They call for the development of a more precise analysis of human behavior and of the relationship between political institutions and social and economic factors. They call for an approach in which politics is conceived as a process that cannot be understood without reference to the contextual factors of a political system.

The Area Focus

Only recently has the study of foreign systems been cast in a frame that carries more promise for comparative analysis. Partly as the result of the war and the need to acquire better knowledge about certain geographic areas, and partly as the result of the intensive and more systematic study by sociologists and anthropologists of human behavior in various non-Western countries, political scientists have become involved in interdisciplinary studies of "areas." An area is a cluster of countries which, because of certain policy preoccupations, geographic propinquity, or common problems and theoretic interests, can be studied as a unit. The political and economic systems, languages, history, culture, and psychology are jointly explored by representatives of various disciplines in universities and government departments. Area studies have developed rapidly in the United States in the last fifteen years. Every big university now has a number of such programs ranging from Western Europe to the Middle East and Africa.[13]

On its face the so-called area programs provide what many students of comparative government consider to be the best laboratory for comparative analysis. For it has been assumed that an area is a cluster of countries in which there is enough cultural uniformity to make the comparative study of political institutional variables between them possible. Furthermore, it has also been assumed that the interdisciplinary approach provides for a more sophisticated and systematic analysis in which the investigator or group of investigators can gain a "total" picture of the system and subsequently be able to dissect it and compare its component elements.

The interdisciplinary approach has suggested some important organizational concepts on the basis of which data could be gathered, variables identified, and comparative study undertaken. Most important among them have been the concepts of *culture* and *personality*. The former stresses the particular traits that constitute the configuration of a culture.[14] Culture-traits or culture-patterns can be identified and compared with each other. Yet in most cases comparison here, even among anthropologists, has assumed primarily the character of pointing out differences rather than explaining them. The *personality* concept on the other hand, by pointing out various personality traits or patterns, provides an instrument for the study of motivational aspects and their variations from one culture to another.[15]

It is difficult to assess the contributions of the area approach to the comparative study of politics. Very often, instead of suggesting a systematic analytical frame within which political scientists might attempt intra-cultural comparisons, the area approach has degenerated into either a descriptive analysis of institutional political structures within the given areas or merely produced monographs in which certain problems were studied with more sophistication with reference to one country. Such books as Robert Scalapino's *Democracy and the Party Movement in Pre-War Japan*, Barrington Moore's *Soviet Politics, the Dilemma of Power*, Alex Inkeles's *Public Opinion in the Soviet Union*, George Blanksten's *Peron's Argentina*, and Merle Fainsod's *How Russia Is Ruled* are the best representative works in area studies, but their excellence lies not so much in their systematic orientation or in the development of analytical concepts for comparison but rather in the sophistication with which the authors relate the political process in the system discussed to the ideological, cultural, and social contextual elements. Institutions are no longer described as if they had a reality which is taken for granted but rather as functioning entities operating within a given context. The descriptive approach gained as a result a richness and flavor which could not be found in the traditional legalistic and historical approach.

But in general, the area approach with its interdisciplinary orientation has failed to provide us with a systematic frame for comparative analysis. For, after all, the very definition of an area is subject to methodological questions with which many of the area specialists never grapple. An area is not a concrete reality as has often been asserted or taken for granted on the basis of considerations of policy or expediency. It is, or rather ought to be, an analytical concept which subsumes certain categories for the compilation of data, provides for certain uniformities which suggest a control situation of the laboratory type within which variables can be studied. Area programs, however, have not attained this level of systematic orientation and as a result their contribution to comparative analysis has been limited. They have enriched our awareness of cultures and institutions in which the political forms vary greatly from the Western forms and they have been suggestive, at least to the political scientist, of the need to broaden his horizon and include in his study of formal institutions many of the informal processes of a system.

CHAPTER TWO

Critical Evaluation
of the Traditional Approach

The preceding chapter presented a general survey of the traditional approach to comparative politics. A brief recapitulation and a critical re-examination are now in order.

Recapitulation of Major Features of the Traditional Approach

The traditional approach addressed itself primarily to Western political systems.

1. It dealt primarily with a single-culture configuration, i.e., the Western world.
2. Within this culture configuration, comparative study dealt mainly with representative democracies, treating nondemocratic systems until recently as aberrations from the democratic "norms."
3. This prevented the student from dealing systematically not only with nondemocratic Western political systems, but with colonial systems, other "backward" areas, and culturally distinct societies which exhibit superficially the characteristics of the representative process (e.g., India, Japan, etc.).
4. Research was founded on the study of isolated aspects of the governmental process within specific countries; hence it was comparative in name only.

The comparative study of politics was excessively formalistic in its approach to political institutions.

1. It focused analysis on the formal institutions of government, to the detriment of a sophisticated awareness of the informal arrangements of society and of their role in the formation of decisions and the exercise of power.
2. In neglecting such informal arrangements, it proved to be relatively insensitive to the nonpolitical determinants of political behavior and hence to the nonpolitical bases of governmental institutions.
3. Comparison was made in terms of the formal constitutional aspects of Western systems, i.e., parliaments, chief executives, civil services, administrative law, etc., which are not necessarily the most fruitful concepts for a truly comparative study.

The comparative study of politics was preponderantly descriptive rather than problem-solving, explanatory, or analytic in its method.

1. Except for some studies of proportional representation, emergency legislation, and electoral systems, the field was insensitive to hypotheses and their verification.
2. Even in the purely descriptive approach to political systems it was relatively insensitive to the methods of cultural anthropology, in which descriptions are fruitfully made in terms of general concepts or integrating hypotheses.
3. Thus, description in comparative government did not readily lend itself to the testing of hypotheses, to the compilation of significant data regarding a single political phenomenon—or class of such phenomenon—in a large number of societies.
4. Description without systematic orientation obstructed the discovery of hypotheses regarding uniformities in political behavior and prevented the formulation, on a comparative basis, of a theory of political dynamics (i.e., change, revolution, conditions of stability, etc.).

A number of factors have accounted for our increasing awareness of the shortcomings of the traditional approach and have led to a reorientation:

1. The prevalent dissatisfaction with the country-by-country approach in teaching and research. The study of foreign governments is not in any sense of the word comparative study. It has been limited, as we have seen, to parallel descriptive accounts of various political institutions and the student is often left to his own devices in noting superficial similarities and differences between political systems.
2. The need to broaden our approach by including in our study non-Western systems and by attempting to relate the contextual elements of any system with the political process.
3. The growing concern with policy-making and policy-orientation. It is probably not untrue to say that research is very often related to the broad exigencies of policy-making. Its global requirements have suggested the close interrelatedness of a number of factors that were considered to be separate in the past and have shown the fallacy of compartmentalization, i.e., of area studies. Yet the need for reorientation is in a sense the natural outcome of the area study programs developed in this country during the war in many universities. Area specialists were brought together and it was natural that they should be asked to relate their findings. This in itself called for comparison.
4. Finally, comparative analysis is becoming increasingly part and parcel of the growing concern with the scientific approach to politics. Science aspires to the establishment of regular patterns of behavior. Such patterns can be discovered only by studying as many systems as possible in the light of common analytical categories.

Probably with the above factors in mind, Pendleton Herring, in his address to the 1953 meeting of the American Political Science Association, stated: "Careful studies that deal comparatively with the cultures and the ideologies, the historical development and the whole complex of forces that seek final expression politically would lead not only to a better understanding of the countries of the world with which we must deal but should likewise enable us to understand ourselves better. . . ."[1]

Critical Re-examination

Re-examination of the nature and scope of comparative study is a relatively recent development. In 1944 a committee of the American Political Science Association, reporting in the *American Political Science Review*, pointed out the need for some methodological reorientation and for undertaking substantive studies of a truly comparative nature. The committee observed:

> In the voluminous material accumulated by the correspondence and the panel discussion, one fact stands out clearly, i.e., that the branch of political science commonly styled comparative government has emerged from a tedious and stagnating routine and, unless this reporter is badly mistaken, is about to undergo a rejuvenation not hoped for by its most ardent devotees—this much to the surprise of those who at first had referred to comparative government as a discipline in a status of suspended animation, hardly alive under the competitive pressure of the more glamorous "international relations" . . . .
>
> Comparative government has ceased to be merely *l'art pour l'art*. It is forced to reorient itself in line with the technological development which is about to weld the world together into a closer union of peoples, if not of states.
>
> Consequently, the majority of the participants in the panel agreed on two basic points: First: comparative government in the narrow sense of descriptive analysis of foreign institutions is an anachronism. As is the case with political science at large, it has to widen its scope to refine and redefine its methods. Second: there is no longer any single technique, neither the orthodox institutional approach nor the strict behaviorist method being sufficient per se to gain access to the true *Gestalt* of foreign political civilizations; methods and designs must be blended and kept in elastic touch and mutual penetration. Although some of the elder statesmen raised their warning voice that *qui trop embracé mal étreint*, that a too promiscuous or ambitious application of diversified methods would lead to dilettantism and confusion, the majority seemed agreed that the frontier posts of comparative government must be moved boldly into the precincts of neighboring and collateral disciplines—that, to use an illustration, criminal law is not under the exclusive jurisdiction of the lawyer if it helps to understand the social function of state and government. The prevailing impression among the participants was that comparative government has lost its traditional character of descriptive analysis and is about to assume the character of a "total" science if it is to serve as a conscious instrument of social engineering.[2]

In a recent report[3] also published in the *American Political Science Review* and incorporating the deliberations of a summer seminar on comparative politics held under the auspices of the Social Science Research Council, the participants agreed substantially with the same general criticisms presented in this study. They, too, felt that comparative study had been comparative in name only; that it was addressed primarily to the Western systems and that it lacked systematic orientation. The authors agreed that the "comparative method revolves around the discovery of uniformities, i.e., the analytical formulation of concepts and problems under which real institutional forms can be compared." Noting that "the nineteenth century students of politics indulged primarily in theories and normative speculations," while "today we have many facts but we do not know why we have them and we are unable to decide what to do with them," they pointed out that it was only by suggesting a scheme of inquiry that systematic empirical research and investigation in the field could be undertaken. Their major conclusion on the method of comparative study and by implication their criticisms of the traditional approach may be stated in full:

1. That comparison involves abstraction and that concrete situations or processes can never be compared as such. Every phenomenon is unique; every manifestation is unique; every process, every nation, like every individual, is in a sense unique. To compare them means to select certain types or concepts, and in so doing we have to "distort" the unique and the concrete.

2. That prior to any comparison it is necessary not only to establish categories and concepts but also to determine criteria of relevance of the particular components of a social and political situation to the problem under analysis (i.e., relevance of social stratification to family system, or sunspots to political instability).

3. That it is necessary to establish criteria for the adequate representation of the particular components that enter into a general analysis or the analysis of a problem.

4. That it is necessary in attempting to develop ultimately a theory of politics to formulate hypotheses emerging either from the context of a conceptual scheme or from the formulation of a problem.

5. That the formulation of hypothetical relations and their investigation against empirical data can never lead to proof. A hypothesis or a series of hypothetical relations would be considered proven, i.e., verified, only as long as it withstands falsification.

6. That hypothetical series rather than single hypotheses should be formulated. In each case the connecting link between general hypothetical series and the particular social relations should be provided by the specification of conditions under which any or all the possibilities enumerated in this series are expected to take place.

The formulation of hypothetical series, it should be pointed out, unlike a single hypothesis (which states what consequence will flow from a given antecedent state X), states series of consequences which will flow from state X or several states, X, Y, Z under particular conditions. It is designed to deal with the problem of verification in social sciences, where the absence of experimental situations prevents us from having sufficiently constant situations to determine the role played in them by specified variables. Under such circumstances we can only state hypotheses for varying conditions, i.e., hypothetical series. The specification of such conditions is what gives us a meaningful element of regularity in the absence of experimental situations and allows us to test our hypotheses by finding not only similar but also dissimilar consequences ensuing from given antecedent conditions.

7. That comparative study, even if it falls short of providing a general theory of politics, can pave the way to the gradual and cumulative development of theory by (a) enriching our imaginative ability to formulate hypotheses, in the same sense that any "outsidedness" enhances our ability to understand a social system; (b) providing a means for the testing of hypotheses, and (c) making us aware that something we have taken for granted requires explanation.

8. Finally, that one of the greatest dangers in hypothesizing in connection with comparative study is the projection of possible relationships ad infinitum. This can be avoided by the orderly collection of data prior to hypothesizing. Such collection may in itself lead us to the recognition of irrelevant relations (climate and the electoral system, language and industrial technology, etc.). Such a recognition in itself makes for a more manageable study of data. *Hence the importance attached by the members of the Seminar to the development of some rough classificatory scheme prior to the formulation of hypotheses.*

The members of the seminar generally rejected the arguments made in favor of uniqueness, and argued that comparison between institutions not only can be made, but also may eventually provide—through types of approach to be indicated presently—a general theory of politics as well as a general theory of political change. Before such theories can be developed, however, it was suggested that research along the following lines must be undertaken in as orderly a way as possible:

1. Elaboration of a tentative classificatory scheme, however rough;

2. Conceptualization at various levels of abstraction (preferable at the more modest and manageable level of the problem-oriented approach);

3. Hypothesizing, i.e., the formulation of single hypotheses or hypothetical series suggested either by the data ordered under a classificatory scheme or by the formulation of sets of problems; and

4. Finally, the constant testing of hypotheses by empirical data in order to eliminate untenable hypotheses by falsification, making possible the formulation of new and more valid ones.

It is regrettable that none of these approaches has been seriously and methodically used by political scientists. Classification is spotty, and, in most cases, of descriptive, formal character. Conceptualization and hypothesizing have not moved beyond the narrow-gauge problem-approach state—and this with reference to the Western European countries primarily. As for a systematic process for the verification and falsification of hypotheses, it remains practically unknown in our literature.

In calling for a new orientation the authors of this report took particular issue with the descriptive character of the traditional approach and with its lack of systematic orientation. The criticisms of the authors, however, were addressed to the method or rather the lack of method followed by the traditional approach, since it would be unfair to assume that they wanted to abandon description of institutional forms or processes! The authors simply pointed out that description does not mean random description. It does not mean the description of a concrete institutional reality simply because it happens to attract the investigator's attention. In fact there is no such thing as description unless we know what we want to describe. One cannot begin with the observation of facts as we are so often told, unless he has a notion of what a fact is, which in itself implies an abstraction made on the basis of certain criteria which are only too often based upon explicit or implicit theoretical commitments. A man jumps from Brooklyn bridge. It is a fact! And yet this very same fact is looked upon in different ways by the physicist, the policeman, the doctor, the psychiatrist, and the man's wife. It is the way in which we look at the phenomenon that makes it an "observable fact." "What are the facts," writes M. R. Cohen, "is far from being clear and self-evident to the naked or untrained eye. Indeed to find all the relevant facts is the final goal of the carefully elaborated procedure which we call scientific method. But discoveries in science are made only by those who know what to look for, and to do this we must have some preliminary ideas as to the way things are connected . . ."[4] This applies with particular force not only to comparative analysis but to the very first step on which we build our material for comparisons: namely, description through which we gain an insight into the institutional arrangements of a system and into the working of the system as a whole.

It should be made clear, therefore, at the risk of overstating the obvious, that the references here to the inadequacies of the descriptive approach are not meant to underestimate the role and significance of description but rather to indicate the need of conceptual categories in the light of which either political systems as such or specific institutional structures and arrangements are described. The dissatisfaction with the descriptive approach does not stem, in other words, from any dissatisfaction with description, which is, as has been pointed out, basic to the study of politics as well as to any other discipline, but rather from the particular manner in which descriptions of Western and non-Western systems were made on the basis of the traditional approach.

Another criticism was that the traditional approach, in its concern with democratic and representative systems, tended to subordinate empirical investigation of political forms and processes to normative standards. Nondemocratic and nonparliamentary forms were treated as aberrations or deviations from the norm and the resulting confusion between empirical and normative study was extremely damaging to comparative analysis and even to description of non-Western governmental systems. For even when nondemocratic societies were studied, the goal of the investigator was to find elements that approximated the democratic forms. This tended, of course, to obscure the understanding of phenomena such as power configuration, legitimacy, and leadership for the sake of describing formal institutions like constitutions and parliaments which in the non-Western systems were very often mere forms whose descriptive study could not advance our understanding of these societies. To the extent to which the apparently similar constitutions that had evolved in non-Western systems were compared with their Western counterparts, confusion became only confounded since such comparison involved invariably two functionally dissimilar political institutions.

Finally, to the extent to which the traditional approach was policy-oriented it suffered from some basic weaknesses. First, the very formulation of the problem calling for a "policy solution" was not made in a manner that indicated the nature of the comparative study involved. Second, the problem was not systematically studied before recommendations based upon comparative study were made. To quote once more the authors of the SSRC Report:

It was agreed that the formulation of the problem should be as clear and logically coherent as possible. A problem selected should be presented in the following form:

(1) The statement and structure of the problem: The problem must be stated precisely; it must be stated in such a form as to lead immediately to hypotheses; it must be analyzed into its component elements; its variables and the relations between them must be spelled out; and all this must be done in operationally meaningful terms.

(2) Its relations to a possible general theory of politics: that is, how would the problem fit into a more general theoretical orientation, and what more general questions can illuminate its solution.

(3) Demonstration of the manner in which the problem calls for the use of comparative method, and analysis of the level of abstraction which comparison would involve.

(4) The enumeration of a recommended research technique for dealing with the problem and justification of the recommendation.

(5) The enumeration of possible alternative research techniques.[5]

Summary

To summarize, the major criticism here of the traditional approach to the study of comparative politics is that it is centered upon the description of the formally established institutions of government; that the expression "comparative government" signifies the study of the legal instrumentalities of government and of political processes conceived as the result of the interaction between the properly constituted organs of government—the electorate, the legislature, the executive, the administration, and the courts; that the traditional approach is in general singularly insensitive to informal factors and processes such as the various interest groups, the wielders of social and economic power and at times even of political power operating outside of the formal governmental institutions, and the more complex contextual forces that can be found in the ideological patterns and the social organization of the system. It lacks a systematic approach. The very word "system" causes a number of people to raise their eyebrows while to others it has connotations of group research that suggest the suppression of the imagination and sensitivity of the observer for the sake of conceptually determined and rigidly adhered to categories. This is far from being the case, however. A systematic approach simply involves the development of categories for the compilation of data and the interrelationship of the data so compiled in the form of theories, i.e., the suggestion of variable relationships. The development of common categories establishes criteria of relevance. Once such categories are suggested, their relevance for the compilation of data through the study of problems in as many political systems as possible should be made. For instance, if it is shown that the composition or recruitment of elites in certain political systems accounts for the degree to which the system is susceptible to change, which in turn may lead us to certain general suppositions about political stability, then a systematic approach would require the examination of the same phenomenon in a number of political systems in the light of the same general categories. While the traditional approach does not claim to be explanatory, a systematic approach claims to be precisely this. For explanation simply means verification of hypothetical propositions. In the field of politics, given the lack of experimentation, it is only the testing of a hypothesis in as many systems as possible that will provide us with a moderate degree of assurance that we have an explanation.

The term "comparative politics" which is favored here in place of "comparative government" is beginning to delineate, therefore, an area of concern and a methodological orientation that differs from the traditional approach. It offers to study the political process and institutions in a truly comparative fashion for the purpose of answering common problems and questions. In so doing it broadens the range of comparison to as many political systems as possible. It abandons the traditional emphasis upon governmental institutions in order to study politics as a social function that involves deliberation and decision-making for the purpose of providing adjustment and reconciliation of the all-prevailing power aspirations. But such a function is neither performed exclusively by the formally constituted governmental agencies nor can it be understood only with reference to the functioning of such governmental agencies. In fact, government is only one of the many factors that enter into the analysis of the political process. In this sense "comparative politics" broadens the range of comparative study by introducing factors that were neglected in the past.

From a methodological point of view "comparative politics" delineates an approach which attempts to identify the characteristics of political systems in terms of generalized categories; it establishes such analytical categories in the light of which identification of political phenomena is made possible for as many systems as possible; it purports above all not only to identify similarities and differences but also to account for them. Explanation, however, requires an exhaustive compilation of data in common categories and the formulation of hypotheses that can be tested. Finally, it aims toward the development of a body of knowledge in the light of which predictions of trends and policy recommendations can be made. In this sense comparative politics becomes a matrix from which theories emerge and at the same time a laboratory for their testing.

CHAPTER THREE

The Need for More
Adequate Conceptualization

The general dissatisfaction experienced by students of comparative politics with the nature of their discipline and more particularly with its methodological orientation indicates the need for a more thorough conceptualization for the purpose of comparative analysis and the development of theories at various levels of generalization for the purpose of organizing and studying empirical data.

The second part of this study will be devoted to the development of a broad frame of analysis for comparative study. But at this stage the writer would like to suggest for purposes of illustration the basic concepts of the scheme. What is important in the categories we shall suggest is their inclusiveness and their utility in helping us collect data which can be used in studying comparatively political problems and institutions. Naturally a particular question or a particular problem may not be encompassed in the categories suggested, in which case the categories will have to be refined or even restated.

Some Basic Concepts

Some basic concepts that suggest a classificatory scheme of politics are the following:

DECISION-MAKING   This is indeed the most universal function of politics, performed by different organs in different systems. It involves deliberation and the formulation of decisions. By deliberation is meant the various forms and procedures in terms of which a political community attempts to meet and solve problems confronting it. By decisions is meant authoritative decisions, i.e., decisions made by certain official organs with the expectation that they will be obeyed.[1]

POWER   This category simply draws our attention to one of the most ubiquitous phenomena of politics: the effort to control or influence the behavior of others. In various systems this will take different manifestations and can be studied with reference to various concrete social forms that can often be suggested in advance. Elites, economic associations, the army, the church, wielders of the communication symbols, and landowners are some of the groups we ought to study in order to gain a picture of the power distribution in a society.

IDEOLOGY   This term refers to the various political ideologies of a system and to the various motivational patterns that characterize the particular behavior of individuals or groups in a system. Its study will often enable us to predict particular types of behavior on the part of individuals or groups within the community.

POLITICAL INSTITUTIONS   By political institutions we understand here both the formal organs of the political community as well as some informal structures which bear upon deliberation and decision-making, such as political parties, tribal organizations, or pressure groups. It is through political institutions that the most important and universal function of politics is expressed—namely, decision-making—at least in a great number of contemporary political communities, and as a result their careful study and description is indispensable.

The interrelationship of the various social and political forces subsumed under the above four categories constitutes the political process. As a matter of fact, we might define political process as the translation of conflict among interest groups into authoritative decisions. In terms of this definition we may consider the power configuration and the ideology of a given society to be the forces that shape the particular conditions under which deliberation and decision-making take place and political institutions are organized. Though they are all mutually interdependent, it is in the power configuration and in the ideology of a system that we shall often find the most dynamic factors that account for change. Yet as they are translated into policy they are altered substantially by the formal organization of institutions and the particular manner in which decisions are made in the system.

The above scheme of reference has a classificatory character. It simply spells out the categories in terms of which data will be collected and arranged. Though it may be based on certain implicit theories about the nature and function of politics and may be oriented toward a functional approach, it does not involve any particular commitments to a theory of politics and as a matter of fact can be used by persons who hold different theories. If we agree that the above categories are adequate for the study of political systems, we may examine the data collected under them or use them for the collection of additional data to answer certain basic questions that will lead to comparative analysis.

For instance:

1. Why do individuals obey a political authority? Under what conditions is obedience to be expected? Under what conditions can we expect disobedience or indifference? What are the most prevalent types of obedience?

2. What are the indicators of tension and conflict in any given system? What manifestations are tension and conflict likely to take?
3. What are the indicators of compromise and peaceful adjustment in any system? What are the manifestations of compromise and peaceful adjustment?
4. What can we say about such elusive things as individual happiness or unhappiness, security or insecurity, well-being or poverty in various political systems?

Undoubtedly there will not be agreement on the concepts advanced here and the questions asked. But this is not so important. *The important thing is where we should, as political scientists, ask questions of this type, questions which purport to apply universally to all political systems, to be equally relevant to all political systems, and to lead ultimately to comparisons between political systems.*

Types of Relevant Theories

Now what particular theoretical schemes shall we use for the study of these questions? Again it is not so important to decide which theoretical scheme to use but rather to use it, and to use it consistently. We may indeed discuss authority, decision-making, ideology, or power in the light of the so-called "group-theory." "The conclusion emerges," writes one of the proponents of the theory, "from the inspection of the literature dealing with the structure and process of groups, that insofar as they are organized groups, they are the structure of power."[2] Another author states that 'the leadership of a society is a criterion of the values by which society lives . . . By learning about the nature of the elite we learn the nature of the society."[3] Thus power is wielded by certain specified groups—the ruling groups—which, according to Professor Lasswell, make the decisions. Or we may adopt the theory of equilibrium that David Easton discusses, according to which, "All elements or variables in a political system are functionally interdependent; and secondly, they will tend to act and react on each other to a point where a state of stability, if even for a moment, obtains."[4] Or we might use a general theoretical scheme according to which there are certain explicit notions about the *functions of politics as a segment of social activity.* Certain functions are indispensable to every system, e.g., the making of decisions, the adjustment of conflict, or the way in which power is legitimized; others are desired by members of the system, e.g., representation of the majority, ascribed stratification or mobility, or the protection of the individual. There are also various modes of performing the functions. Again, some such modes have to be found in all political systems, e.g., the hierarchical organization of power or the process of selecting elites. Others are specific to certain systems for particular purposes, e.g., parliamentary institutions or elections. Here the central accepted scheme lies in viewing politics as a social function and political forms as structural variables that can be compared.[5] Or we could use the Marxian theoretical scheme for comparative study, or that of Durkheim, according to which systems are analyzed on the basis of complexity, i.e., the degree of differentiation of functions.[6] Our purpose here is simply to show that theoretical schemes exist and that all that counts is to use them consistently for the purpose of analysis and explanation.

Theory and the comparative study of politics become, therefore, inseparably related. The first attempts to isolate and identify the most significant variables in terms of which empirical data observed in all systems may be interrelated. It calls for the establishment of propositions that interrelate various phenomena of politics. It suggests areas of relevance by postulating broad frames of reference within which political systems are studied. The second undertakes the empirical examination of such propositions, their reformulation and the ultimate reconsideration of the frame of reference originally postulated. This is no division of tasks properly speaking but only a logical separation of the two aspects of comparative politics.

The Range of Comparison: Units and Variables

The particular questions we ask, our conceptualization, and the particular theory we have postulated will often determine the range of comparison. By range we may understand either the number of countries we shall include in our comparison or the particular number of variables we have included in our theory. Thus the range is determined in advance by the interests of the investigator. The study of political change, for instance, under the impact of Western influences in the various colonial areas involves a multitude of variables and a great number of countries to be studied comparatively. The impact of an electoral system, on the other hand, upon the number of political parties in Western democratic societies involves a smaller number of variables.

The range of comparison depends on the level of our abstractions and the comprehensiveness of our theory. For the student of comparative politics will invariably have to relate a particular theory either for the purpose of proving it or disproving it to an ever-increasing number of conditioning factors in terms of which such proof or disproof can take place. For instance, supposing we search for the factors that account for the multiparty system in France. Such factors will have to be stated in hypothetical terms that will call for empirical testing. We may relate the multiparty system with the French electoral system. Once we do this, comparative analysis will reveal the existence of a similar electoral system in another country without multipartyism. So that we shall be immediately forced to relate multipartyism in France to another conditioning factor—regionalism, for example. Again, however, comparative study may indicate that regionalism and an electoral system similar to that of France exist in another country side by side with a two-party system. At this point we shall be forced to redirect our attention to France and search for a third conditioning factor which, coupled with regionalism and the electoral system, accounts for the multiparty system. This may be attributed to the characteristics of certain groups to remain independent and refuse to coalesce in larger groupings—something that will again call for comparative explanation. However it may be, the burden of comparative analysis is invariably that of tracing a phenomenon to a number of conditioning factors whose interrelationship becomes imperative in terms of the comparative study we undertake. A relationship of factors A, B, C, D, E, and F, for instance, may indeed account for a political manifestation in a given country whereas in another country a different manifestation may be due to the interrelationship of factors A, B, and E. The search for conditioning factors whose presence or absence accounts for certain phenomena and the verification of the relationship between such conditioning factors in terms of comparative empirical observation is the very essense of comparative analysis and determines the range of comparison. It is only through such a process that we can hope to find *ultimately* causative factors and erect a general theory of politics.

We compare, therefore, in order to discover the conditions under which certain phenomena take place. Conditions—or, more precisely, a series of conditions—are analytical devices that are hypothetically related to the phenomenon we study. The task of empirical observation is to test the validity of such hypothetical formulations. By so doing we enrich our knowledge of the conditioning factors that account for a given phenomenon until the time comes when we shall be able to put these conditioning factors into a generalized frame or scheme and then the presence or absence of some or others will enable us to make tentative predictions about political phenomena.

Static and Dynamic Comparison

We attempt to compare phenomena in the light of a set of conditioning factors. Comparison here may be either static or dynamic. In the first instance we undertake a careful analysis of the most prevalent political forms and institutions. We undertake an anatomy, so to speak, of political systems. We identify and describe structures and point out their relationships. Certain significant and universal concepts of politics have already been suggested. The meticulous description of the corresponding institutional structures through which such functions as deliberation or decision-making can be identified is of great importance.

It should be pointed out, however, that description of various structures in the form of classificatory tables need not remain at the all-inclusive level of a total description of political systems. It may be directed to the description of a process or even the descriptive presentation of phenomena that are to be found only within a regional "area" or even in one or two countries. The decision is in the hands of the investigator and will be determined by the question he has asked and the interests he has.

The great number of descriptive works we have on legislatures, constitutions, and civil services are indeed a storehouse of information—but they constitute only the very first step toward comparative study. A much more sophisticated analytical scheme and classificatory table of an aspect of politics—elites and the phenomenon of leadership—is to be found in the recent *Elite Studies* prepared at Stanford.[7] Here the detailed description of the composition of elites not only suggests unsuspected similarities between systems that were considered to be heterogeneous and therefore unamenable to comparison but also suggests fruitful hypotheses and points to the existence of certain general conditioning factors that are radically transforming the character and nature of leadership to a great many political systems.

Concrete structures, however, and their variables must be carefully identified for what they are. That is, they must be identified in terms of the particular function they perform in a system. This is much more difficult than it may seem to be. Like the sociologist, we must discern the overt from the covert functions and the manifest from the latent ones. For instance, though there are striking structural analogies between the electoral system of the Soviet Union and that of the United States, comparison breaks down when we compare their functions. They are wholly dissimilar. The function of elections in the United States is an integral part of the decision-making process over which the body politic becomes divided. In the Soviet Union, on the other hand, elections have a ritualistic function. They are used to express loyalty to the regime; they unite the people around the policy of their leaders or the symbols of authority. They perform a function similar, in broad terms, to the July 4th celebrations in this country.

The second part of comparative study, therefore, is what we may call that of *dynamic comparison*. It is the study of processes and the performance of functions of various systems. Here we attempt not only to identify structures through which certain functions are performed but also *to account* for the concrete structural variations between systems. It is at this stage that we attempt to do three very important things in comparative government: (a) *account* for similarities in the light of analogous conditioning factors, e.g., a two-party system and a majority electoral system; (b) *account* for differences in the light of different conditioning factors, e.g., a multiparty system and a single-member majority electoral system and ethnic minorities; and (c) *attempt to predict* future occurrences in the light of a chain of conditioning factors that we have identified. This last stage is indeed the most significant one but at the same time the most difficult to reach.[8]

The Problem Approach in Comparative Study

The possibility of comparing political systems in terms of some of the most important functions they perform and the attempt to broaden the range of comparison to as many systems as possible may at this stage be premature. It may be preferable to compare certain processes or institutions or certain factors that are included in our over-all scheme rather than use the scheme itself for the purpose of making total comparisons. By the same token it is more advisable to limit comparison to geographic or cultural areas in which certain uniformities are assumed and in which the number of variables to be related is therefore smaller. For that matter it might be even more constructive to delimit the number of variables and the number of countries in which they will be studied comparatively by *the formulation of problems.*

The problem approach is susceptible to a variety of formulations ranging from a very high to a low level of abstraction. The study of political instability, for instance, as a "problem" defines highly general and abstract contours of empirical observation, classification, and hypothesizing. On the other hand, the study of political instability in parliamentary systems requires a more limited degree of conceptualization and has a more limited range of observation and variables. Finally, the study of cabinet instability in its relation to electoral systems is a "problem" of a relatively lower degree of conceptualization and abstraction and includes an even more limited range of variables.

The problem approach is often divided into two main categories: (1) The theory-problem approach, in which the problem is suggested by particular theoretic or methodological considerations. This type of problem approach is in turn divided into (a) the middle-range theory-problem approach and (b) the narrow-gauge theory-problem approach. (2) The policy-oriented problem approach, in which, as we shall see, the problem is suggested by concrete manifestations of conflict or instability and its study is related to the need of adopting policies that will do away with the cause of instability or conflict.

THE MIDDLE-RANGE THEORY PROBLEM APPROACH   This approach requires a theoretical scheme involving a fairly high degree of generalization and abstraction but remains below the level of a general and comprehensive scheme of politics. In the words of Robert K. Merton, theories of the middle ranges are "theories intermediate to the minor working hypotheses evolved in abundance during the day-by-day routines of research, and the all-inclusive speculations comprising a master conceptual scheme from which it is hoped to derive a very large number of empirically observed uniformities of social behavior."[9] The selection of problems and their formulation may aim at the development of a comprehensive theoretical scheme. This is not, however, the most important objective of the middle-range theory approach.

THE NARROW-GAUGE THEORY APPROACH   Narrow-gauge theory involves the selection of a problem that may be studied with reference to a very limited range of variables and hypotheses. Though it fulfills some of the same functions as middle-range theory in providing for classificatory schemes for the collection of data, and in suggesting hypotheses, it differs fundamentally from it in the following respects: (a) it is confined to a very limited range of variables; (b) it can be used only for the study of phenomena in closely similar social contexts; and (c) the hypotheses formulated are postulated primarily for purposes of falsification, since a narrow-gauge problem approach will always be falsified by the introduction of new conditions and factors. As a result, narrow-gauge hypotheses can be used only with the understanding that their function is to suggest broader theoretical formulations.

The most familiar narrow-gauge hypotheses are those used for the study of Western political systems. They pertain to the study of the relationships between cabinet, parliament, political parties, and electoral systems. Though such hypotheses have often been formulated, they have not been used systematically for comparative study. The reason has been that they have been uniformly "disproved" and, as a result, abandoned in favor of a descriptive study of uniqueness. To give an illustration: Does the power of dissolution create well-disciplined parties which in turn account for cabinet stability? The question as formulated obviously relates to the parliamentary systems of Western Europe. Empirical observation may reveal that there is a missing link in the relation of the above hypothesis, namely the *electoral system*. Hence the problem to be hypothesized about may be reformulated in the following terms: Does the power of dissolution in a single-member-district majority system bring about party discipline and cabinet stability? On the basis of comparative study an affirmative or negative answer may be unwarranted, first, because no two parliamentary systems of Western Europe satisfy the proposition, and second, because, even if they did, stability in the one system and instability in the other might be the rule.

The most important functions of the narrow-gauge theory approach, therefore, is that, through a process of falsification rather than "proof," it trains students to think and study in terms of hypotheses and eventually to learn how to relate the study of politics with broad social, economic, and cultural contexts of given systems, i.e., to increase the number of the conditioning factors that account for various phenomena.

A POLICY-ORIENTED APPROACH   A second type of problem approach, emphasized recently by a number of authors,[10] is the presentation and selection of problems for the purposes of policy formulation. Both in their selection and in their study, problems are related to the requirements of policy-making. They are selected because of "conflict situation" or "high degree of tension." They are studied for the purpose of suggesting "solutions" through which the causes of tension may be alleviated or removed and through which conflict may be eased. For instance, the occupation of Germany by Allied troops for a long period of time was deemed to be a "solution" to the perennial problem of German military nationalism. It was a long-range proposition, aiming at the destruction of some of the most tenacious symbols associated with German history. It appears today, however, that the concern of the policy-makers with the solution of this particular problem was somewhat misplaced and that the problem of German nationalism should not have been considered outside of the context of Soviet nationalism and of the requirements of European economic reconstruction.

The above illustration, one among the many that may be given, indicates one of the dangers of the single policy-oriented problem approach. Conflict and tensions are the result of many interrelated conditioning factors and situations in the context of a dynamic time dimension. A solution that is addressed to one of the causes or to a single configuration of causes may provoke new problems and bring about unanticipated consequences. It is doubtful, therefore, that the policy-oriented approach can be divorced from a systematic and theoretical study of tension, conflict and change.

Two difficulties should be kept in mind, therefore, in the problem-oriented approach: first, that of defining the boundaries of the problem, and second, that of setting it within the proper time dimensions. To begin with, the cluster, or what we call the conditions that define the problem, requires a clear definition. This, in turn, means the establishment and formulation of clear-cut categories under which facts pertaining to the problem may be collected and classified. Furthermore, the same applies to the host of other interrelated phenomena. Interrelatedness, however, is a problem requiring systematic formulation of conditioning factors, which means that we have to establish meaningful relationships. Colonial revolutions, for instance, may well be the product of Western ideology and technology. It would logically follow that the withdrawal of Western influence and practices might alleviate the intensity of the conflict situation. Revolution and nationalism in China, however, are related not only to Western techniques and ideas, but to a new pattern of class and power configuration, to conflicts around myths of authority and legitimacy, and to the present international situation. A great number of "causes" of "conditions" must be studied before we can begin to get an insight into the nature of the Chinese revolutionary movement and be in a position to offer what we may consider to be a "solution."

Similar considerations should be kept in mind with reference to the second difficulty, namely, the setting of interrelated facts within a time dimension or a time factor. This also required the prior elaboration of a theory of change. Otherwise, short-range "solutions" may indeed prove to be self-defeating, while long-range policies may fail to bring about any of the desired results.

The policy-oriented problem approach might be encouraged, therefore, with the following reservations in mind: (a) The possibility of studying a single problem in order to administer a "solution" should be avoided. A problem should be placed in its proper setting, i.e., together with a number of other interrelated problems. This is the task of theory. (b) A cluster of problems should be carefully defined with reference to their boundaries. This is again a matter of setting up relevant relationships. (c) The introduction of the time dimension is of crucial importance for both the understanding and the "solution" of the problem. This calls for a careful elaboration of a theory of change based upon extensive empirical investigation.

Criteria of Relevance

The formulation of problems and the empirical investigation that takes place within the frame set by them raises some serious questions. How are problems to be selected, for instance? The problem approach, if detached from a theoretical scheme, may lead to excessive randomness and, if it is an integral part of a theoretical scheme, may suffer from the limitations inherent in the scheme. Are problems, then, to be stated on a simple ad hoc basis, and are they to reflect solely the investigator's imaginativeness and sensitivity? And once problems have been selected, how will they be formulated and presented? Are they simply to be couched in terms of the interest of the investigator, or does the latter have the responsibility of pointing out the nature of the problem with reference to some broader theoretical considerations and of the significance of his expected findings? These questions are raised because the recent trend towards empirical investigation has lost a great degree of its significance through the reluctance of the investigator to point out the relevance both of his problem and his questions, as well as of his findings, to political science. Very often data is accumulated after long surveys with no clues to its significance. Collective and individual research of this type—both in comparative politics as well as in political behavior and public administration—though empirical, does not advance the cause of an empirically-oriented science. Our purpose is not to collect facts but to study them only when they can yield answers to questions.

There are a number of criteria that can be used for the selection of a problem. Policy-oriented problems are formulated, as has been pointed out, because of the pressing need for action or the demonstrable existence of conflict and tension. A study of racial relations in major urban centers of this country, for instance, is in a sense comparative and attempts to elicit information and data that may guide policy-makers. Insecurity and its manifestations under various political and economic systems is a problem that can be studied comparatively and is again formulated because of the observable signs of tension. Studies of revolution undertaken comparatively may shed light upon the relevant factors that bring about violent action by certain groups. Such studies may be undertaken either for the purpose of examining a phenomenon as such or for the purpose of eliciting policy-action in order to avoid the recurrence of the phenomenon we study.

The problem approach has, therefore, the great advantage of orienting research empirically along multiple avenues without being tied down to grandiose and premature theoretical schemes. Its flexibility and adaptability to modest levels of empirical research at manageable levels of abstraction is its greatest merit. The problem approach may be directed toward the study of political change, ideology, motivation, political structure, and political functions. So long as research satisfies the elementary requirements of relevance and logical coherence, it will throw light upon the areas that have remained singularly outside of the purview of the political scientist, and will modify our thinking and interests: (1) It will increase our awareness of the relationship between political, social, and economic factors. Comparative study here should attempt to isolate the most significant contextual elements of a system and relate them in the form of a problematic approach to the political process. (2) It will train the political scientists to test the analytic value of comparison. When we are faced with the question of "verification" our answer cannot be given in terms other than comparative. (3) Through a process of elimination of the irrelevant, it will suggest meaningful relationships.

PART II

COMPARATIVE POLITICS: A SCHEME OF ANALYSIS

CHAPTER FOUR

A General Scheme for Comparative Analysis

Problems of Analytic Schemes

Every student of politics has an implicit or explicit scheme of analysis. Such a scheme is often nothing more than a series of concepts with which the student attempts to order the political reality he is observing. In many instances, the student does not feel obligated to tell in advance what his questions are, in what categories they are put, or how they are related to each other. De Toqueville's *Democracy in America*[1] is an excellent illustration of this procedure. We know that De Toqueville is concerned with "what is Democracy and how it works in the United States." In the course of his discussion, he raises a number of significant questions and attempts to give some answers: What are the characteristics of the democratic system? What are the most significant ideological elements of a democratic system? What forces may cause a democratic system to negate its basic prerequisite, freedom? To what extent can the system be transplanted into other societies and under what conditions can it be expected to function? The reader will find in this analysis a remarkably clear-cut listing of the various conditioning factors under which American democracy functions and a speculative evaluation of the various factors that guarantee the viability of the system or endanger its existence.

The student of comparative politics is naturally concerned with the development of a scheme of analysis that will be comprehensive and that will indicate relevant categories for the compilation of material. This part of our study will attempt to construct such a scheme.

An analytical scheme should be formulated in such a way as to be applicable to as many political systems as possible. This calls for the development of general and abstract analytical categories in the light of which particular phenomena and institutions in as many countries as possible can be studied and whole systems compared. To give an illustration: Most comparisons have dealt with concrete institutional structures—parliaments, political parties, bureaucracies, and the like. Assumed in such comparison is the notion that the functions of seemingly similar institutions in different countries are comparable, that the institutions themselves correspond to analogous processes. This, for instance, is the case when the Supreme Soviet is compared to the American Congress or when "elections" in the Soviet Union are compared with elections in the United States or England. The same is naturally true when comparisons are made between the one-party system and multiparty or two-party systems. A better way to proceed is to study these institutions and processes in the light of abstract analytical categories descriptive of functions.

The formulation of questions calls, therefore, for an a priori conceptual design. It should be pointed out, however, that given the present state of political science, there is no such conceptual design and every student is free to develop his own concepts. His only obligation is to formulate them as clearly as possible and to show their relevance and superiority to other concepts on the basis of (1) their generality and (2) their analytical utility in identifying concrete institutional realities in terms of the functions they perform or of the particular processes to which they correspond.

The Political System: Four Categories of Analysis

For the purpose of illustration a scheme will be developed here composed of four basic analytical categories in the light of which political systems can be studied and compared. They are the following: (1) the deliberative process and decision-making as a function of politics; (2) the power configuration and its social and political aspects; (3) ideology and its role in political motivation and institutional organization; and (4) the organization of political authority. This conceptual frame can give us relevant categories for the study of both political morphology and political dynamics. We shall try here to analyze each one of the categories suggested, to illustrate their utility for the study of structures, and to indicate their importance in the study of the operation of a system.

The above categories are selected for a number of reasons. First, they stem from the theoretical assumption that the essence of politics is to be found in the deliberative or the decision-making processes through which power aspirations and conflicts—perhaps the most ubiquitous raw material of politics—are reconciled. Second, they suggest the general supposition that politics is a universal phenomenon to be found in almost every society and that it is channeled through concrete specialized institutions. Some of these institutions are formally recognized and known, as is largely the case in the Western political systems, but others are merely informal arrangements or nongovernmental structures in which political, religious, and economic functions may be combined. The association between paterfamilias and the king, or between the chieftain and the state—between *patria postestas* and *imperium*—is an illustration of such undifferentiated stages. We are witnessing today, however, a progressive development toward "politicization" in most of the former colonial areas, including Africa, whose most important characteristic is the growth of specialized institutions performing political functions. The deliberative and adjustive process takes place through institutional structures that are increasingly identified as political. The arrangement of these institutions often determines the nature of the organization of political authority.

Decision-making and the various deliberative processes are manifested through institutional political structures. They are intimately related to two other foci of our system—power configuration and ideology. The concept of power suggests the need of studying carefully the system under observation for the purpose of finding the particular ways and means through which men or groups of men attempt to control and influence the lives of others or to control or influence the decision-making process in the system. This calls for the enumeration of a number of subcategories that will help us to observe and study the manifestation of power relations in the system and to relate them to the political institutions and the decision-making process. At the same time, to understand the deliberative and decision-making process in a system we must know its ideology. Ideology is used here to cover the beliefs and the various motivational patterns of the society, i.e., the operative ideals of a system and the manner in which they have crystallized into institutional patterns.[2]

The categories suggested are broad enough to help us study any particular system. They are equally suggestive for the formulation of theoretical propositions. For instance, the formal political arrangements in a system very often mirror the existing power relations while at other times they do not. In some cases the political institutions and the deliberative process are responsive to the power aspirations of various groups, while in other cases they are not. The observer may, with the use of the above categories, isolate the variables that account for such differences. Variations, for instance, may be sought and found in the particular organization of a system or in the particular motivational pattern of the society. They may be due to the intrusion of a foreign ideology and the particular susceptibility of the political leaders to it.

In addition to the opportunity they offer for the study of problems and the comparative analysis of variables, the categories suggested help us differentiate between political systems as such. The organization of political authority varies but it is only by using ideology and power configuration together with the institutional arrangements for decision-making that we may get an analytical picture of the differences between systems and of the way in which these differences affect profoundly such problems as political consensus, stability, and change.

CHAPTER FIVE

The Political System: Decision-Making

Politics involves the performance of certain social functions. The making of decisions for the attainment of certain purposes—adjustment of conflict, change, adjudication—is probably the most prevalent social function of politics. Political decisions are, however, those which emanate either from authorized persons or from organs which are known and recognized by the community. The use of sanctions to enforce the made decision does not constitute a unique characteristic of the political process. Otherwise, the decisions of a corporation to increase prices and its ability to use sanctions for the maintenance of such process could be called political. The characteristic phenomenon of politics is the legitimization of force, the development of a state of mind among the members of the community according to which decisions made by certain organs or persons are, generally speaking, obeyed. This opens up some interesting areas for comparative study that will be considered later, but at this stage it indicates the close relationship between ideology and decision-making.[1]

Decision-making is the most pervasive function of politics. It can be discovered in any political system from the traditionalist systems ruled by custom to the constitutional systems in which the process becomes identified with rational procedures. The forms and types of decision-making vary from one system to another and the content or the area of decision-making is also a matter that shows significant variations between political systems.

Decision-making is an analytical concept which involves a set of questions or categories in the light of which concrete institutional realities can be identified, described, and compared.

Who Makes the Decisions?

In every system we shall find persons or organs through which decisions are made. The chieftain of a primitive tribe, the medieval courts, the administrative official in a modern democratic state, the legislatures—all make decisions. We very often associate the decision-makers with the political elite of a given system and this is generally correct provided we understand clearly that there is a difference between political elites and other kinds of elites. If we define an elite as the "wielders of power and influence,"[2] then we shall have to indicate in every comparative study we make whether the political elite is the *real* elite or not. We may well find, in other words, that the officials or the organs that are ostensibly responsible for the decision-making process are mere puppets manipulated by other groups. In such a case, the understanding of the location of political power involves the careful study of the relationship between the political elites and the actual wielders of power. The question of who makes the decisions cannot be resolved therefore by an examination of a system's constitution or formal legal structure. Very often we have to unearth the persons or groups of persons that control or influence directly the formally recognized officials who seem to make decisions.

How Are Decision-Makers Selected?

Each system has its own particular way of selecting political leaders. There are, however, some general categories under which all forms of selection can be classified. In some societies, the mode of selection is *ascriptive*, i.e., it depends upon the status and birth of certain individuals. In other societies, selection depends upon *achievement*, the demonstration of individual effort and capacity. Charismatic leaders and many of the elected officials in a democratic society are of this second type. In other political systems, including very often democratic systems, selection depends upon a combination of ascription and achievement. This was the case, for instance, with nineteenth-century England, and the House of Lords continues to demonstrate the existence of some vestiges of an ascriptive mode of selection.

The mode of selection of decision-makers differs, as has been pointed out, from one political system to another. It would be interesting for comparative study to attempt to develop certain meaningful hypothetical relationships between various systems and elite structures, and to attempt to get a general notion of change through the study of modes of selection and the conditions under which one elite gives place to another. Are we to expect, for instance, as a general rule that the development of new skills or division of labor will cause an ascriptive mode of selection to be replaced by one based on achievement? If so, what will be the impact of such a change on the organization and the stability of the political systems?[3]

Composition of Political Elites

Political leaders in any particular society exhibit ideological traits and skills that should be carefully studied for the purpose of comparative analysis. More particularly, it is relevant to ask whether they belong to any identifiable social or economic or religious group, whether they are identified with a particular region, whether they use symbols and media of communication alien to the rest of the population, and what techniques they employ to wield power and maintain their position of leadership.[4] Here again the study of the various symbols and techniques used by political elites is extremely important for the purpose of comparing them with reference to the performance of their respective systems. A comparative study of the composition of a political elite and the symbols and techniques it uses will often throw much more light upon the differences or similarities between two systems with reference to decision-making than a comparative study of their formal political organs.

In many systems the formally and legally established political leadership does not actually make the political decisions. In such cases, the location of the real power to make and enforce decisions should be sought out and studied. We ought to study the qualifications of the actual wielders of power, the channels through which they operate, the reasons why they refuse to assume a recognized and formal position of political leadership, their relationship to the political elites, and their modes and techniques of control.

Wherever, therefore, there is a difference between the real and apparent wielders of power, the student must face and attempt to answer a number of questions. The first is simply: Why the differentiation? The second question is the significance of this differentiation with reference to the dynamics of the system—namely change, adjustment, and the achievement of goals. The third one relates to the over-all performance and stability of the system, for if actual power is divorced from legal recognition, it might be at least hypothetically inferred that the system is either highly traditional and stable or that it is highly unstable, involving a continuous conflict between the formal political elites and the real decision-makers.

The Deliberative Process

Decision-making is normally preceded by the deliberative process. In every political system certain procedures can be found through which decisions are arrived at and articulated. In some societies, ritual and religious symbolism often hide the actual procedures of consultation and deliberation. Sometimes highly ritualized procedures are important in securing compliance and enforcing decisions. In charismatic leaderships, the source of the leader's power and the means for securing compliance are often confused with the procedures through which decisions are made. Both the Nazi and the Soviet systems, though stressing the charismatic nature of leadership and using the personality of the leader to secure compliance to decisions, use highly rational techniques for reaching decisions. There is nothing irrational or intuitive, for example, about the way in which the five-year economic plans are drafted in the Soviet Union.

The discussion of the means by which decisions are made can be clarified by identifying certain decisions in the order of their significance and attempting to relate them to the processes through which they are arrived at and to the concrete political units through which they are articulated.

Kinds of Decisions

There are, to begin with, certain *fundamental decisions* that affect the position of the decision-makers themselves as well as the whole pattern of decision-making in a given system. Sometimes such decisions are made on the basis of prescribed processes, i.e., a constitutional amendment, such as the Reform Act of 1832, while in other systems such over-all decisions are made through nonprescribed techniques such as a revolution. An extremely important aspect of comparative analysis is to determine in advance the existence or nonexistence of prescribed forms for fundamental decision-making in any political system. For there is prima-facie evidence that constitutional and democratic systems in which fundamental decisions are made by formal processes involving the participation of the bulk of the community are, generally speaking, less susceptible to violence and revolution than systems where fundamental decisions are not made by recognized processes or are left in the hands of small political elites.

A second type of decision are those we usually refer to as *legislative enactments*. They affect the status and the rights of many persons in the community and they establish new techniques and procedures for the making of decisions in the community.

A third type of decision are those affecting a small number of persons or individual cases. Such decisions are actually of an *administrative or judicial* type, and in most instances they correspond to techniques through which decisions of the second type are made applicable to specific cases.

Decisions of the second and third types are related to certain concrete political institutions in any given political system. Legislative decisions are made by representative assemblies, political parties, the electorate, or by other established organs, such as a council of elders, a priesthood, or the body of tribal warriors. The task of the student of comparative government is to identify the particular political organs and procedures through which such decisions are made before attempting to compare them. To assume, as is often done, that all legislatures or all representative assemblies make such basic decisions and that they are, as a result, comparable is to be deceived by appearances. We may find that some comparative studies of concrete political institutions that have been assumed to make basic decisions, such as the British Parliament and the U. S. Congress, are essentially misleading; the legislative function of the British Parliament is, in fact, of secondary importance.

It must also be made clear that when we attempt to identify the institutions and processes through which decisions are made we ought to include all the organs that we can identify irrespective of where we find them. A comparative study of the Soviet Union and the United States should attempt to relate the Party structure and procedures for decision-making in the former with the Congress and the President in the latter. In other words, the institutions through which basic decisions are made differ in various systems, and comparisons must be based on actual functions rather than on appearances. By the same token, the study of the army or the church or of economic associations from the standpoint of decision-making may yield important findings for the understanding of the phenomenon of decision-making in a given system.

It is also necessary to attempt to discuss the manner in which various types of decisions are made in a system and to analyze in some detail the deliberative process. All types of decisions involve some kind of deliberation ranging from direct consultation between the decision-maker and his consultants in a simple despotic system to the elaborate co-operative studies made by a network of functionally divided agencies in a complex bureaucratic system. In fact, the differences between authoritarian and democratic systems with reference to the decision-making process is often a matter of degree.

Steps in the Deliberative Process

The deliberative process involves two steps: (1) the formulation of a problem; (2) the clarification of the problem with reference to other issues facing the society.

FORMULATION OF A PROBLEM   A problem requiring a decision emerges in various areas of social and political life. A depression, the impossibility of maintaining high production quotas because of poor skills in the labor force, the demands of certain groups for the satisfaction of newly felt wants are some of the many factors that can be responsible for the creation of a problem. In different systems problems are defined in different manners. In a democratic society the press, various associations, religious and economic groups constantly confront the properly constituted agencies of the government with new problems. In authoritarian systems, the party often performs the same function. Its members are sensitive to people's reactions and they are very quick to transmit reports of discontent or positive suggestions to the higher echelons of the party. So much attention has been paid to the control aspects of the party in an authoritarian system that very little study has been made of this particular function. In other systems, particularly in traditionalist societies, there are no channels for the formulation of problems. In fact, in such societies the very emergence of a problem requiring deliberation and decision has an explosive force that undermines the cohesiveness of the social and political institutions. The introduction of Western technology in various colonial areas is an illustration of this phenomenon which is only too clearly perceived in our days, particularly after the withdrawal of the stabilizing control exerted until recently by the colonial powers.

The process of discussion and examination of a problem, after it has been raised but prior to the formulation of a decision, which is really at the heart of the deliberative process, takes a number of forms depending

upon the type of political system in which the problem emerges. Sometimes deliberation is limited to the political elite; at other times deliberation brings the existing political elite into conflict with newly created social
and economic elites, as was the case prior to the French Revolution. At
times the emergence of a problem splits the political elite into two camps,
each vying for political leadership and control. The emergence of a problem
in that case may lead to violence or to a broadening of the participation of
the members of the community in the deliberative process since the elite
groups vying for control have often to appeal to the community for sup-
port.[5] But in either case, the emergence of a problem has revolutionary
implications involving either a challenge to the existing political leadership
of the system or the pitting of one type of elite against another.

The persistence of a problem situation which presses for articulation
and formulation may leave the existing political leadership apathetic until
the gulf between it and the bulk of the community becomes so deep that
nothing but violence can result. This was the case with the French nobility
prior to the French Revolution and more particularly with the Russian
ruling classes throughout the nineteenth century. Their typical reaction to
the existing problems was one of increasing differentiation from the
masses of the people—in manners, language, and political orientation.

CLARIFICATION OF THE PROBLEM   The clarification of a problem takes
various forms. In a democratic system, problems are debated through every
available channel of communication. The press, the radio, the schools and
universities, and various pressure groups try to relate the problem to other
issues facing the society. The political parties attempt a more precise formulation which gives an opportunity to the bulk of the community to choose
between alternative solutions. In authoritarian, one-party systems the party
attempts to do the same thing, though the community is hardly offered
a choice between conflicting viewpoints. In this case, however, the party
performs a function remarkably similar to that performed by the varied
free agencies in democratic systems. It assists the population in a deliberative process in which the problem is thrashed out. The basic difference is
that the party never gives to the population an opportunity to accept or
reject the solution arrived at. In other systems, the process of clarification
is restricted to a small group of consultants or to the bureaucracy or takes
the form of magic and divination.

Legislatures have traditionally played a very important role in the deliberative process. For once the contours of the problem are defined by the
parties or through other formal and informal means, a sharper formulation
and ultimately the making of a decision is needed. The legislative bodies
reflecting the opinion of the community attempt to clarify the problem,
to relate it to other existing problems, and to suggest a solution. But at the
same time—and this is primarily a recent phenomenon—an increasingly
complex network of institutions parallels the task of the legislative bodies:
advisory committees, the bureaucracy acting through hundreds of func-

tional committees, and specialized bodies—scientists, economists, and various experts—participate in the discussion of the particular problem. The role of the expert and his intrusion into the deliberative process is one of the most significant developments of our day. In all technologically advanced societies there is a constant interplay between legislator and bureaucrat, between politician and expert, between interest groups and various functional committees. In many instances, this interplay is not haphazard but well institutionalized. In other cases, particularly those involving deliberation in new problem areas, the interplay is unorganized. Comparative study addressed to this question will again show that there is a marked similarity between political systems that have been traditionally considered to be dissimilar—such as, for instance, the deliberative process in Nazi Germany and in England, or in the United States and the Soviet Union.

Before we come to the discussion of the content of a decision it would be worthwhile to note that in a number of political systems the raising of a problem is no longer a matter of political agitation or party initiative. A number of administrative agencies define problem areas on the basis of study and documentation. There are, in other words, rational techniques for the identification of a problem in a modern advanced society—administrative agencies, groups of experts, *ad hoc* appointed committees, and special executive agencies. A comparative study of these institutional arrangements will throw light on some of the new institutions developing in a number of contemporary states and will show their significance and relationships to the other institutions of the state.

The Contents of Decisions

Decisions made by any of the political agencies of the state under the general terms discussed above affect the status and interests of groups and individuals and, in certain instances, affect the rules pertaining to the decision-making process itself. Decisions may be divided, as we have seen, on the basis of their substantive character into a number of categories, in the light of which they can be fruitfully compared.

There has been a noticeable shift in the content of decision-making in the political systems of most industrially developed countries toward an increasing regulation and control of economic and social rights and conditions. Whereas the nineteenth-century political systems were primarily concerned with the enunciation in general terms of abstract political and individual rights, such as the right to vote, there has been a growing concern recently with the implementation of rights through actual control and manipulation of social and economic factors in the system. At the same time, decisions are being made not for the whole community or the body politic in the form of broad rules applicable to all, but rather for specific groups, specific problems, and particular aspects of the social and economic processes. The decisions, therefore, have tended to become increasingly specific and technical in content. Such decisions tend to create a very complex system of rights and expectations on the part of groups in the society so that many political systems are drifting into a situation where social and economic status is often determined in terms of legal categories to which certain groups belong. Status is increasingly becoming not a matter of birth or occupation but rather of a relationship between identifiable groups of citizens and legal enactments that provide specialized treatment for them.

CHAPTER SIX

The Political System: Power

A second general category under which data should be collected and carefully interpreted for the purpose of comparative study is that of power. The pursuit of power by individuals or groups is, like decision-making, one of the most universal characteristics of social and political activity. The paterfamilias, the priest, the chamber of commerce, the landowner, and the entrepreneur not only seek and exercise power over certain other human beings but attempt to entrench themselves into positions from which social and political power can be effectively wielded.

Political power must be defined not in terms of influence or domination or control but in terms of authority. It is that segment of social power which is exercised by *recognized* and *accepted* organs to achieve certain commonly shared objectives and purposes of the society. Power, as we have seen, has been transformed into authority through the use of the appropriate political ideology and institutions. It is, generally speaking, the power exercised by the state and its organs, though it is likely to find some of its characteristics in systems where there is no political organization like the state.

But though "political power" can be differentiated in the above terms from other forms of social power, it is manifested within the totality of the social power configuration of a given system. Political power is surrounded, so to speak, by other elements of social power, by other groups and associations all of which attempt to influence its exercise and to bend it to their own particular interest or purpose. To the extent to which other power-motivated groups attempt to exert direct or indirect influence upon political authority and its organs they enter the picture of political analysis and become part of a scheme that can be subjected to comparative study. It would be impossible, for instance, to discuss political power in a given system without reference to organized groups such as labor, industrial associations, religious groups, tribal organizations, and the like. Their organizations and structures, the intensity of their activity to influence the centers of decision-making, their techniques of action, and their particular ideologies are all factors that must be taken into consideration by the student.

Group Theory and the Theory of Class

Two broad theories have been developed for the purpose of relating
social groupings endowed with social power to the political process and
decision-making: the *group theory* of politics and the *class theory*, both of
which may be used for the purpose of comparative analysis.

GROUP THEORY   The group theory postulates that decision-making is the
resultant of the activity of organized groups. They all impinge on the
decision-making process and more generally on all aspects of the deliberative process and the sum total of group activities becomes translated into a
decision.[1] According to this theory, the reality of politics is hidden below
the surface of the properly constituted and recognized organs through
which decisions are articulated. It is hidden in the continuous struggle for
power and influence upon which groups are constantly engaged.

Comparative analysis can be fruitfully pursued in the light of this theory
by isolating in various systems some groups and comparing their relationships to the respective political organs of the system. No a priori statement
as to which groups we should select and observe can be made, though the
study of the American system throws some light on the importance of
some groups. The groups to be studied are generally economic interest
groups, professional associations, religious groups, special purpose groups
(i.e., veterans). The impact of these groups upon political activities and
processes should be studied in various countries in terms of a number of
key factors: their national or regional character; their general or specialized character; their structure and membership; their leadership and resources; the techniques they use to mobilize opinion; their relationship to
political parties or to other quasi-public institutions; the degree of internal
autonomy and the nature of their internal organization. With reference to
their techniques of action, particular attention should be given to the secret
or open way in which they act; to their attitude to violent action; to their
efforts to use persuasion rather than pressure; to their dependence on
foreign powers.

It is equally important to attempt to study the ideology of the particular
groups within a society. To what extent is there an acceptance of the
common political ideology by all groups pursuing power? To what extent
is there a fragmentation of legitimacy because of sharply contradictory
ideological conflicts between groups? To what extent do we find a tendency among groups to compromise their differences by participating in
nation-wide political groups such as the political parties or, conversely, are
groups entrenched in a particular locality or attached to a particular ideology in such a manner as to make their ability to participate in general
purpose activities unlikely?

The student of comparative politics is at a great disadvantage here because there are no adequate studies of groups and of their relations to the

political process or political ideology in any system outside of the United States. Yet the use of group theory may indeed cast new light upon the comparative study of at least Western institutions and our first task is to identify and describe the various groups in Western European countries, to say nothing of the non-Western system for which the applicability of the theory itself may be questioned. At this stage, therefore, the group theory can be used for the purpose of collecting data and material under new categories rather than as an explanatory theory. It is too difficult to use the theory for the explanation of certain political phenomena or of similarities and differences in various political systems without first getting a clear notion of what may be called the "ecology" of groups in various systems.

CLASS THEORY The theory of *class struggle* which is an integral part of Marxist doctrine has been in part discredited because of its rigidity and its identification with dialectical materialism. For all practical purposes it may be argued that the Marxist theory has not been borne out by historical developments because the political organs of a number of Western systems have altered significantly the class configuration and class conflict. But despite this, the class concept might be useful for comparative study at least with reference to some political systems. For instance, it would be most unfortunate to attempt to understand and describe the revolutionary process in Russia in the early part of the twentieth century or the French Revolution of 1789 without making use of the class concept. It would be equally unfortunate to try to understand some Western and non-Western systems such as, for instance, the Latin American political systems or those of Japan or India without the use of the concept of class.

The class concept proposed here is in fact a variant of the group theory. It simply postulates that at certain times and under certain conditions a number of groups tend to coalesce in order to protect certain common interests and values or to challenge a given set of values. It is a concept that applies with particular force to systems in which we do not find some of the prerequisite conditions we associate with a democratic system—freedom of debate, political parties, implementation of social goals through orderly decision-making, freedom for various groups to present their points of view and attempt through persuasion to influence decision-making. In default of such institutional arrangements groups gravitate toward a center that is generally determined by economic interests and this center represents what we may loosely call a class. It is the common denominator of various claims that cannot find free expression. This is a phenomenon naturally associated with systems that lack institutionalized forms for peaceful change or with a situation of rapid change or radical transformation of leadership. It manifests itself with particular clarity on the eve of the breakdown of the political institutions of a society rather than in the course of their normal functioning. As such, it has both *objective* and *subjective* characteristics. The objective characteristics can be found in the polarization of groups on the basis of economic criteria and interest such as income, land ownership, capital ownership, occupation and the like. The subjective characteristics, on the other hand, can be observed in the political ideology and the political elites. We shall find a convergence of a number of group ideologies into two ideological patterns, the one defending the status quo while the other challenges it. Such ideological polarization is an indication of crisis, reflecting a temporary coalescence of a number of groups and new points of view which find expression in common action and in the development of a new doctrine.

Another subjective element associated with class configuration to which more attention has been paid recently is that of *leadership*.[2] The human element here—the subjective factor—that provides the leadership can come from any particular group of the society. Family ties, group affiliations, pecuniary motives are swept aside and persons who normally would be expected, because of their family ties and economic interests, to provide the leadership for the class that defends the status quo are often found on the opposing side, whereas unemployed and disinherited may fill the ranks of the elite that supports the status quo.

The class concept, therefore, is an analytical tool of particular value in the study of revolutions and rapid technological innovations that disrupt the pattern of social life and lead to the establishment of a new system of political and social relations. Rather unsuitable for democratic societies in which the institutions and political process provide for agreement, change, and reconciliation of conflicting interests, this concept of class can be used with better results for non-Western systems as well as for societies undergoing rapid change.

The Instruments of Power

In a number of systems, particularly non-Western political systems, the instruments of power and control are usually to be found outside of the frame of the existing political institutions. Very often such political institutions as may be identified are mere organs in the hands of a class which maintains itself in power. They are not instruments for the mitigation of conflict between various economic and interest groups but rather instruments for the elimination of conflict through force. The more force is used, however, for the maintenance of the interests of certain groups, the more we find a tendency on the part of the disfranchised groups to coalesce. The more such groups coalesce, the greater the intensity of force employed by the holders of power. The phenomenon of polarization of the society into groups, those who defend the status quo and those who challenge it—that is, the phenomenon of class conflict—becomes clearly apparent in any such society.

Some of the instruments of power in the hands of such groups are the following: (1) land-ownership; (2) the army; (3) the church; (4) the means of communication; and (5) complete dominance of the deliberative and decision-making process. Each of these instruments is naturally safe-guarded by the legal system, by a restricted basis of recruitment into the ranks of leadership, and by direct legal disabilities imposed upon groups that do not participate in the control of any of the above instruments of power. In such systems there is hardly any doubt that the holders of the instruments of power can be identified as a "class" and the same applies to the bulk of the community that is dissociated from such instrumentalities of power. The division of the society into power-holders and subjects is paralleled almost invariably by the division in the allocation of the resources of the given community. The power-wielders are the "haves" and the subjects the "have-nots."

CHAPTER SEVEN

The Political System: Ideology

The third broad category of the analytical scheme proposed here is that of political ideology. By political ideology is understood the patterns of thought and belief related to the state and the government that constitute at one and the same time a source of obedience and consent and a mechanism of control. As De Toqueville writes, "without such common belief no society can prosper; say, rather, no society can exist; for without ideas held in common there is no common action, and without common action there may still be men, but there is no social body. In order that society should exist . . . it is necessary that the minds of all the citizens should be rallied and held together by certain predominant ideas."[1] To put it briefly, the role of political ideology is to legitimize the organized force of the state.

The phenomenon of legitimacy is a universal phenomenon of political life and no comparative study between political systems can take place without a clear appreciation of its role. A legitimate authority is one where "force has been transformed into right and obedience into duty." It is precisely the role of the political ideology to accomplish this transformation.

Ideology naturally refers to the whole complex of motivation and pattern of behavior that characterizes a society. As Professor Lowenstein puts it, "An ideology is a consistent and integrated pattern of thoughts and beliefs, or thoughts converted into beliefs, explaining man's attitude toward life and his existence in society, and advocating a conduct and action pattern responsible to, and commensurate with, such thoughts and beliefs."[2] Political ideology, however, refers to the same patterns of belief and behavior that are related to the decision-making agencies of the system and to the manner in which the power configuration of the society is shaped and the relations between power groups established.

There are four significant aspects of ideology to which comparative study can be addressed: (1) the source of the dominant political ideology; (2) the diffusion of ideologies, an aspect which pertains to a range of problems such as the acceptance of an ideology, the mode of diffusion, the modifications brought about in a system by the impact of alien ideologies; (3) the function of ideology as an instrument of social control; and (4) the relationship between ideology and the organization of political authority in any given system.

The Sources of a Dominant Political Ideology

Myths and values that shape social and political conduct obviously emerge either within the system or are borrowed from outside in one way or another. The process of borrowing may be due to imitation or imposition or assimilation; it may involve a selective acceptance or rejection and it may result in a synthesis in which indigenous and foreign values are fused into a single pattern.

Political myths emanate from certain groups in the society and they slowly become accepted by the bulk of the community. What are the specific groups that develop a political ideology? Is there a close relationship between the elite groups of a society and the ideology which is developed? If so, what is the pattern of dissemination and acceptance? What are precisely the characteristics of these elite groups that develop an ideology until it becomes dominant? Is it skill? Ownership of land? Occult knowledge? To what extent is the existing political ideology a rationalization of the dominant position of a class, as Marx argued? Can we, in general, attribute the prevalent political ideology to dominant interest groups within a given system?

It is the task of the student, therefore, to identify the existing ideological pattern in a given society, and to attempt to trace it to the particular dominant groups from which it originates and to assess its general content and effectiveness. With respect to this latter point, it is necessary to examine the techniques through which the existing ideology is maintained. The school system, the use of media of communication, the particular methods of propagation—coercion, intimidation, inculcation—are extremely important. Finally, an examination of the existence of competing political ideologies within a given system is of great relevance for the purpose of assessing the strength or weakness of the political leadership. For one of the clearest indices of instability in a given system is the existence of political ideologies that are either hostile to each other or are incompatible.

The relationship between ideology and the dominant groups of a society suggests a number of questions. What is the relationship between the type of group and the content of an ideology? How do changing economic conditions affect the predominant groups and their ideology? Conversely, what is the impact of ideology upon group stratification in a given society and its relationship to social and economic changes? When can we accurately talk about a "rigid" ideology, one that resists change? What are the characteristics of an "elastic" ideology, one that can accommodate itself to new patterns of thought and change?

Diffusion of Ideologies

It is probably a truism to say that political ideologies have a tendency to spread from the area in which they were developed to adjacent areas, to lose some of their original characteristics in the process, and to blend with the ideological traits of other areas. History reveals clearly the impact of some of the political ideologies of the Greeks upon Rome, of Rome upon the Western world, of the United States upon the Latin American countries and upon the Asiatic world, of the Soviet Union upon some Eastern European and Asiatic countries. Such an expansion is naturally organically related to social, economic, and power factors. But in all cases, it takes place through a process of selection and rejection whereby only certain elements of a given ideology are being accepted and other elements rejected.

We have very little knowledge of the conditions that account for this process. For instance, in Latin America we often find in one and the same country elements that can be traced to the Indian culture, to Spain, and to the United States. In nineteenth-century Russia, the pattern of belief and action that separated the ruling class from the peasants or the intelligentsia could be traced to a rather intricate pattern of acceptance and rejection of Western European ideologies by the ruling group. The reception of Marxism and democratic liberalism in a number of the colonial areas reflects an equally intricate and obscure process of acceptance and rejection.

A number of hypotheses can be formulated for the purpose of ordering and exploring this process of ideological diffusion. It may be assumed that geographic affinity is the most important conditioning factor for the diffusion of ideology, and that economic and military power is an indispensable condition, and that similarity in economic conditions makes the diffusion far more likely. Or it may be argued that the conditions of rejection and acceptance, when we look at the matter from the point of view of the recipient country, depend upon the internal stability of the system.

It may be hypothesized, for instance, that a well-integrated political system will be more resistant to outside ideologies than an unstable society, or that a prosperous society in which there is equitable distribution of wealth among its members will be less receptive to outside ideological influence than a society in which there is poverty or a sharp division in the distribution of wealth. It may be finally argued that the nature of the political system itself is an important conditioning factor accounting for reception or rejection. If there is a sharp division between power and responsibility or between the ruling class and the masses of the society, new ideologies will be more readily accepted either by the ruling class or by the masses.

The Intellectuals

In almost all cases, comparative analysis here ought to be focused upon the most sensitive social and political groups through which ideologies are maintained and propagated or, as the case may be, challenged—the intellectuals.[3] The study of the intelligentsia in any society may well prove to be the best indicator of the stability of a given political ideology, or, conversely, of the receptivity of the system to new political ideologies. The intellectuals manipulate the ideological symbols of a given society. The teacher, the writer, and the priest are some of the channels through which power becomes translated into legitimacy and the governors thereby linked with the governed. A number of criteria about the role of the intellectual in a given society may lead us to some significant conclusions about the internal cohesion of the system and its reactions to different ideologies. The social status of the intellectuals, the degree and extent to which they are valued by the society, their political and economic status, their relationship to the governing class, and the responsibility they have for the performance and the maintenance of the system are certainly definite and observable criteria on the basis of which we may foresee with a fairly high degree of accuracy the susceptibility of the system to foreign ideologies and to internal change.

A far more difficult problem, but one imperative for policy-orientation, is the study of a situation in which a country is exposed to two conflicting ideological systems. This is the situation today in a number of former colonies that have acquired independent status and are exposed to Western and Soviet ideological influences. Could we surmise on the basis of concrete social, economic, political, and historical determinants the impact of the two ideologies? Naturally, this is not so much a problem of studying the rejection or acceptance of one or the other ideology in toto but rather of speculating as to which political ideology will exert a preponderant influence on the given country. Where shall we look for an answer? To the class structure? To the various social and political elites? To the intellectuals? To the tenacity of the existing symbols and myths? To the particular social division of the society with reference to the existing distribution of wealth? To the historical past of the country which in itself reveals certain patterns of behavior? There is hardly any doubt that all these factors enter into our scheme of analysis and that they should be carefully considered in any empirical investigation by the student of comparative politics before he attempts to develop any more elaborate theories. They should be advanced in the form of problems on the basis of which studies of specific areas can be made before we attempt to generalize and compare. The questions suggested here simply indicate possible interrelationships. Some of them may be modified in the process of empirical investigation and data-gathering and new and more relevant ones may be formulated.

Political Ideology and Political Control

As already indicated, in this discussion political ideology is identified with legitimacy, with the myths and symbols that make it possible for the political elites of a given society to govern. The effectiveness of a political ideology is therefore commensurate with the degree and intensity of its acceptance. Indeed, one of the most important indicators of the lack of control in a given society by the political elites is the lack of an effective political ideology, or the existence of a number of conflicting ideologies.

Not enough attention has been paid to the control function of ideology and no adequate comparative study of this function has been made. The Marxist assumptions that the prevalent ideology of a given society is fashioned by the ruling class, i.e., the class that owns the means of production, and that the state is established for the protection of the interests of this class, have not been adequately tested primarily because of the extreme form in which the Marxist thesis was originally cast. Yet a broad survey of political institutions and ideologies indicates that ideologies are related to the dominant economic and social groups. New ideologies are evolved either to challenge the existing pattern of economic and social relations and subsequently to challenge the myths and symbols of the political elites, or to buttress the claims of another social group to political power. The French political scene after the Revolution of 1789 is a series of struggles for power in which political ideology is formulated and employed in these ways. The Marxist ideology, in turn, as adopted by the Russian intelligentsia and a small part of the working class, challenged the prevailing power structure of Russian society and later became the ideological weapon that buttressed the claims of the Party for absolute political control.

Given a relationship between social and economic classes and political elites, and given the assumption that political ideology is an instrument through which political leadership gains acceptance by the bulk of the community, a number of questions remain to be explored. These questions are related primarily to the power configuration of a given society and to the political institutions through which ideology becomes crystallized.

Political Ideologies: A Typology

Since the function of political ideology is to legitimize power or challenge the existing power relations, it has a direct bearing upon the organization and structuring of political institutions in a given society. In a broad sense, political ideology determines a number of the characteristics of a political system such as the allocation of status, the performance of services, the definition of the relations between individuals and groups operating within a given society, the patterns of motivation of the society, the degree of individual participation, and, conversely, the areas of what we might call political apathy. It is in this sense that a typology of ideologies is possible. Any such typology, however, it should be noted, will abstract a great deal from actual types, so much so that we shall be dealing with ideal types, since very often elements pertaining to different ideologies can be found to exist in a given system.

Professor Lowenstein, in the article referred to,[4] distinguishes the following types:

1. Absolutism, as monarchism, dynasticism, legitimism, or with a more religious accent, as theocracy and Caesaro-Papism

2. Constitutionalism, institutionalized in the ideologies of representative government; parliamentarianism; the rule of law (*Rechstaat*) and democracy

3. Individualism, in both economic and political implications, as liberalism, free enterprise, capitalism; humanism

4. Social collectivism, as either democratic or proletarian socialism (communism)

5. Nationalism; imperialism; racism; internationalism; universalism

6. Elitist and organistic ideologies, such as aristocratism; agrarianism; managerialism; corporativism, and the modern variants of fascism.

This listing is indeed too general for the purpose of comparative study, though each of the ideologies indicated represents certain significant patterns of institutional configuration. In some cases like racism or proletarian communism, they represent myths of an overwhelming force that shape political institutions and political action. Nor is it possible to compare between ideologies as such without the use of certain general but at the same time identical criteria. We might use the position of the individual and the existence or absence of individual rights; we might, in a more narrow sense, use the distinguishing characteristic of the deliberative process in a given political system; we might take the criterion of decision-making processes (e.g., arbitrary, tyrannical, absolutist, constitutional, democratic); we might take as a criterion the economic function of the state (e.g., collectivism, socialism, individualism). In all such cases, the important factor is the formulation of general criteria that can be applied to as many systems as possible, the identification of existing ideologies on the basis of these criteria, and the comparison between them with reference to political institutions and, finally, the evaluation of the intensity of an ideology in terms of its integrative or control function in the system.

CHAPTER EIGHT

The Political System: Institutions

Political institutions are social instrumentalities for the attainment of certain kinds of community goals. The relationship between the institution and its function constitutes the political process. Though from an analytical point of view structure and function are differentiated, the study of the political process is the study of the interrelationship of the two.

The political process defined as the translation of conflict into decisions naturally takes a great variety of institutional forms in various systems. The function of decision-making, for instance, which involves a deliberative process, may be performed by distinctly dissimilar structures—e.g., the soothsayer and the priest, a council of elders, the leader and a narrow circle of followers, one political party, two political parties, elections at regular intervals with full participation of all the members of the community, a federal system, or a parliamentary system. At the same time, identical structures or institutions may perform different functions. For instance, the legislative chambers in France, England, and the United States perform functions which, upon closer observation, will be found to differ radically. In a number of instances, institutions that used to perform certain functions slowly shift to the performance of other functions or become mere symbols with a ritualistic character. Kingship is a typical example of the latter development.

In the comparative study of political institutions and processes, we may adopt patterns of inquiry that involve different levels of abstraction. We may attempt to compare systems on the basis of the organization of political authority as Max Weber suggests.[1] We may compare certain institutions with reference to functions, such as decision-making, adjustment, change, or communication.[2] We may attempt to compare specific institutions that are parts of a process, such as the legislative assemblies, the bureaucracy, the political parties, the executive, the roles and status of individuals, and the legal system—all with particular reference to individual rights. No matter what the level of comparative study, the requirements of our analysis are the same. We must identify the structural unit performing certain functions and study a process.

The study of processes, however, may also involve different approaches. The student may proceed to describe an institution without a detailed analysis of its function. From this point of view, as we have pointed out earlier, meticulous description of an institutional structure is extremely important. Detailed knowledge of the structure may ultimately prove to be of great help in understanding its proper function. Or we may choose to describe and analyze certain functions performed by an institution without attempting an exhaustive descriptive analysis of its structure. We may describe social security or welfare measures and compare them to similar decisions in other systems without comparing in detail the social structures through which these functions are performed.

Criteria for the Classification of Political Systems and Institutions

Political scientists have attempted to classify political systems according to certain basic criteria that have stood the test of time and can be quite useful for comparative study. Such criteria are related to: (1) the organization of political authority; (2) the relation between the established political authority and the members of the community; and (3) the position of the individual.

THE ORGANIZATION OF POLITICAL AUTHORITY The complex of institutions that constitute the organization of political authority is referred to as the state. Though the term has fallen into some disrepute, it still has great utility. For the state is indeed an inclusive concept that covers all aspects of policy-making and enforcement. The main weakness of the concept, for the purpose of comparative study, however, is precisely its inclusiveness. To compare the British "state" to the French "state" would indeed be synonymous to comparing the political systems of the two countries.

We may avoid the difficulty by referring to the "governments," a term which expresses the concrete institutional organization through which the most important political functions, namely decision-making and enforcement, are performed.

The Organization of Political Authority and Decision-Making Certain general types of governmental organization may be defined with reference to decision-making. For instance, Max Weber's three types of authority depend on whether decisions are made on rational grounds, traditional grounds, or charismatic grounds.[3] These three types correspond to different patterns through which decisions are made. In the first case, decisions are made through a highly differentiated apparatus of government involving established and accepted procedures of conduct and an organization of structures based upon community recognition; in the second, decisions will be made only in terms of conformity to certain traditional or customary rules of conduct. In traditional types, we shall find little differentiation of the governmental structure, little application of knowledge to the making of decisions. Finally, in the charismatic type

of authority, decisions flow from the leader without any appeal to knowledge or to tradition and without any development of institutionalized
channels through which the decision must be expressed in order to receive
acceptance.

Enforcement of Decisions   Political systems employ various means
through which decisions become enforceable. Enforcement is closely cor-
related with the degree of acceptance of an institution or particular decisions by the community. As long as the particular institutions or process
through which a decision is made are respected, there is every expectation
that the decision will be generally obeyed. This is the case, for instance, to
refer again to Max Weber's categories, with a constitutional system, or a
traditional system, or even a charismatic system as long as the charisma
lasts. Obedience is due in the one case to the fact that procedures are
valued or because tradition or the charisma has established patterns of
loyalty or obedience. But again, it is likely that at a certain point a decision
may be challenged or not be obeyed. When we have a series of cases where
decisions are disobeyed, we have a direct challenge to the decision-making
institutions as well. The performance of a political system viewed from
the standpoint of decision-making can be assessed, therefore, with reference to a number of objective criteria such as compliance, extent and
types of noncompliance, the loss of prestige and the weakening of legitimacy claims on the part of the decision-making organs.

The organs that enforce decisions are easily recognizable in any political
community—the police, the judiciary, and numerous administrative authorities which appear under different forms and names in various degrees
of complexity and diversity in various societies. Again, the prestige they
command, the claims to legitimacy that they can validly make, are indicators of the performance of the political system. Conversely, the weakening of prestige and legitimacy indicated a potentially unstable or revolutionary situation. This can be viewed both *internally* (i.e., the extent to
which the enforcement organs in a community implement their function)
or *externally* (i.e., the extent to which the community at large treats the
enforcement organs with deference or at least recognizes their claims to
command). At the point where the "external" and the "internal" elements
are absent we clearly have a revolutionary situation. "The Cossacks riding
through the streets went through all the apparent motions of suppressing
riot," writes John Maynard, "but a junior French diplomat took note of
a trifling incident. He saw a Cossack wink to one of the rioters."[4]

Enforcement and Ideology   From what has already been said, it is
apparent that one significant element of enforcement is the value pattern
of the society as a whole with particular reference to the acceptance of
the decision-making organs and the decision-enforcing organs. This, as
has been indicated, can be studied with reference to legitimacy and to a
number of objective indices in terms of which compliance can be
measured.

It is equally plausible, however, to attempt to study the same phenomenon with reference to the concept of political leadership and other forms of social leadership. Leadership depends in essence upon its ability to command respect and recognition. The methods used vary, but the most common ones are *myths* and *persuasion*.[5] As with almost every other process touched upon here, comparative study should explore these methods in detail, relate them to other elements of the social and the political process, and attempt to draw generalizations with reference to effectiveness, political stability or instability, and peaceful change. It has recently been argued, for instance, that political leadership is slowly changing its techniques and changing, too, in its composition. Leaders of persuasion are slowly giving place to leaders of coercion, which, in turn, leads to a complete transformation of the organization of the political authority.[6] Only detailed comparative study can illuminate this problem. Similarly, comparative study of the transition of elites that relied upon coercion to elites using persuasion might throw some light on the process and its significance. Comparative studies of ancient societies or primitive groups would indeed be very fruitful here.

RELATIONSHIP BETWEEN ESTABLISHED POLITICAL AUTHORITY AND THE INDIVIDUAL   Another important criterion for the comparative study of institutions and processes is that of the relationship between the individual and the state. A number of categories can be used for studying this relationship and it is quite likely that only when we have assessed their particular significance and their interrelationships will we be able to come up with some fruitful generalizations about some of the political phenomena already mentioned: stability and instability, change, and achievement of social goals.

Recruitment   The relationship between the individual and the organized political authority may be studied with reference to the mode of recruitment of political leadership. To what extent is leadership openly recruited? To what extent is recruitment based upon certain conditions? To what extent is recruitment limited to considerations that are unrelated to individual effort or ability? The study of the political leadership in England as compared to that of the French aristocracy throughout the eighteenth century will suggest some important differences. The impact of the extension of the franchise upon political leadership in various countries again offers us a good experimental situation for comparative study.

Education   The relationship between the members of the community and the established political authority can take a number of forms. The least investigated of all is what may be called the _apathy_ of the bulk of the community toward political authority and the particular groups that wield power over it. This is characteristically the phenomenon that we observe in the great majority of the Latin American states, and, to some extent, the same phenomenon was observed among American Negroes for some time after the Civil War. In the great majority of cases, apathy can be traced to historical factors such as the exclusion of a conquered people from participation in the political process, to ethnic and racial factors, to sharp cultural differences between the leadership and the rank and file, and to educational and linguistic differences.

The reverse of apathy is, of course, the direct participation of an entire community in all decisions. This is often the case with small, primitive, homogeneous, tribal communities, or occasionally with advanced communities of a small size in which the level of education is high and the degree of class differentiation relatively small, as in Athens for a few decades before the Peloponnesian War.

Between these two extremes, we have situations in which relationships between the established political authority and the members of the community range from apathy through various degrees of participation. Such variations are largely due to the level of education of the members of the community.[7] It may indeed be advanced as a general proposition that the higher the level of education of the bulk of the community, that is, the more diffused the mastery of skills and communication symbols, the higher the degree and intensity of participation. The political forms and the character of participation may vary here, but this same phenomenon can be observed in democratic as well as authoritarian societies. It most definitely cannot be observed, however, in aristocratic, military, or traditional societies.

Political Participation   The participation of the individual in decision-making is a separate criterion for comparative analysis, and it should be studied with reference to both the formal structures of a system as well as to some of the informal arrangements. The student of politics should examine:

1. The constitutions and existing institutions. Such matters as the electoral system, the right to vote, limitations upon the freedom to vote should be studied comparatively in two or more systems.

2. Provisions concerning the eligibility of candidates.

3. The process of nominations. If he finds that eligibility and nominations depend upon certain conditions that involve discrimination against some, the student can conclude that there are rigidities in the system which make it likely that participation will be open to some but not to others. For instance, the nomination of a candidate in elections in the Soviet Union is controlled by the Communist Party. This is prima-facie evidence that participation is restricted.

4. Whether or not more than one party exists. The existence of more than one party generally indicates wider participation of members of the community than when there is only one party.

5. Whether the systems being compared allow associational freedom. The freedom to belong to associations of various types is often directly related to the freedom to have more than one political party. The existence of many associations is again prima-facie evidence that participation is free to many members of the community. But as with the political party, the student should inquire into the ways in which associations are formed and act. If he discovers that their formation and action is dependent upon government authorization and that such authorization involves discrimination against certain political, religious, or

cultural groups, he can conclude that participation is not open and free. The Soviet Union, for instance, has what appears to be a very vigorous associational life. On closer observation, however, we find that these associations are entirely controlled by the political authority.

6. The available information and knowledge on the basis of which citizens are asked to make decisions and participate in the decision-making process. To the extent to which information about social and economic problems or about foreign policy is withheld, participation is hampered. Again it will be the task of the student of comparative politics to identify the most significant institutions that provide information to the members of the community and to compare them as to impartiality, effectiveness, accessibility to the public, and the like. It is equally important to undertake the task of discovering the persons or groups in charge of the various instruments that disseminate information. Finally, the role of the government in disseminating information should be studied and evaluated since there has been a uniform tendency, at least among most Western European governments, to establish specialized agencies to collect and analyze data and present it to the public.

7. The institutions through which the responsibility of the persons in the government can be assessed and enforced in some way. We associate responsibility with those processes that render the decision-makers accountable to the community and provide the community with political and legal sanctions. Political sanctions involve periodic elections, legislative review with the possibility of censure or removal, and financial control by a representative assembly. Election is an important sanction, or rather instrument, for insuring effective responsibility only when it is possible for groups and political parties to criticize openly the persons wielding political authority.

THE POSITION OF THE INDIVIDUAL   The position of the individual in the system is another important criterion for classification and comparison. Traditionally, political speculation has dealt with many intangible values centering on the individual and his position in a given system, such as "justice" or the "good life." These terms, slippery as they may be, in the sense that they involve ethical categories, continue to preoccupy the student of politics and a fortiori the student of comparative politics. In fact, as has already been pointed out, one of the most important contributions comparative government can make is to indicate through the comparative study of institutions the proper type of corrective action for the realization of certain value goals. Laswell writes:

How do we go about inventing and evaluating hypothetical constructs? Our reply: Select according to goal values. The grounds of this advice are the characteristics of rational thought. Rational thinking takes the consequences of its own exercise into account. Among the factors moulding the future are interpretations of the future. Since expectations have an impact, however modest, upon policy, we proceed rationally when we operate with a clear conception of our possible effect upon the shape of things to come . . . Without introducing an extensive treatment of values at this point, we submit the following anticipatory comment: We are concerned with the dignity of man. We want to participate in the realization of human dignity on the grandest possible scale.[8]

This writer does not propose to give here any recipes for how the dignity of man can be realized! We are primarily concerned with the criteria that can help us to get a picture of the position of the individual in any given system. Some such criteria have already been discussed with reference to the relationship of the individual to the established political authority. There are others, however, that should be mentioned.

The test of any system is the opportunities it provides to the individual to live peacefully with his fellowmen, that is, internal security and the development of institutions for the adjustment of individual and group conflict. A political system should provide men with opportunities for employment and economic security as well as for political participation. This means that the system should provide for education and freedom in the widest possible sense of the word—freedom of thought and expression, religious freedom, and freedom of association and political action. Above all, men must be treated by the government on a footing of equality. This means that they should not be differentiated on any basis other than ability and achievement; it also means that no handicaps should be placed for any reason whatsoever upon the potentiality of a man's development.

To translate these principles into measurable or at least researchable propositions for the purpose of comparative analysis is a difficult but by no means impossible task. A survey of the legal systems of a number of countries may reveal, for instance, the existence of legal disabilities or the degree to which the courts are accessible to all, irrespective of education or ability to pay. It will, in fact, indicate whether the system is in general motivated by a concern for the individual or whether it tends to subordinate the individual to the interests of the state or to certain political and social groups. The study of party structures will indicate the extent to which individuals can voice their opinions, participate actively in the nomination of candidates, or themselves run for office. The study of communication systems will indicate the degree of control by public or private persons and whether and how the systems are used to propagate the dominant political ideology. A comparative study of the distribution of national incomes in a number of systems may suggest that in some the individual share varies so greatly as to give to a few a disproportionate advantage over others. The comparative study of educational systems will show that in some societies the development of skills and the acquisition of knowledge is limited to a minority; or it may indicate that, though the acquisition of skills and knowledge is being made accessible to all, education is not used for the free development of individual initiative and thought but rather as an instrument through which conformity to the dominant ideology is being inculcated.

A Typology Based on the Foregoing Criteria

The organization of political authority, the relations between the established political authority and the members of the community, and the position of the individual in a political system are comprehensive categories that can be used for the classification of various systems and for comparison between various forms.

ORGANIZATION OF POLITICAL AUTHORITY AND DECISION-MAKING On the basis of the way in which authority is organized for the purpose of decision-making, we may distinguish between various contemporary forms such as federal and unitary systems, or those characterized by separation of powers and fusion of powers; between military dictatorships, presidential and parliamentary regimes, authoritarianisms of various types, aristocracies, monarchies, and democracies.

After identifying the various systems on the basis of formal channels of decision-making, we might refine our classification by attempting a typology for the various institutions that would include the organization of the legislative structure, the institutional arrangements of the executive branch of the government, the growth of the bureaucracy and its particular institutional arrangement, the organization of the judiciary and its participation in the decision-making process and the electoral processes.

We may further attempt to refine our classification by studying the organization of one of these instrumentalities for decision-making for the purpose of identifying different types. For instance, a detailed descriptive account of various legislatures calls for a study and a description of the procedures and rules of debate, the mechanics of law making, the role of the speaker or president of a parliamentary assembly, the committee system, and the position of the private member.

Once we have identified the various institutional units and have assessed their parts in the decision-making process, we should attempt to gain a picture of the whole process. What are the relations between the executive and the legislature? What are the relationships between agencies of the bureaucracy and the legislature? What role do legislative committees play in decision-making?

RELATIONSHIP BETWEEN COMMUNITY MEMBERS AND POLITICAL AUTHORITY This second category is more inclusive than the first. The constitutional arrangements, either written or unwritten, that specify the pattern of relationship should be studied and departures from the written provisions clearly indicated.

In general, if we group the electoral and nominating process, the existence or not of associational and party freedom, accessibility of the individual to information, and finally, the responsibility of the wielders of political power to the community and the institutions through which such a responsibility is implemented, we shall be able to suggest a satisfactory classificatory scheme of a comprehensive nature. Thus, in an authoritarian system, we shall find that the electoral and the nominating functions are enforced in such a way as to enable the wielders of political power to exercise a virtual monopoly over elections, which in turn helps them to perpetuate themselves in power. The formal institutions become in an authoritarian system instruments of control rather than channels through which decisions are made and responsibility enforced. The party mechanism is not only an instrument for the recruitment of political leadership and for gauging and molding public opinion, but also the exclusive instrument for the formulation of policy and for control. Responsibility of the governors to the bulk of the community for their policies is not institutionalized. The political leaders are responsible to the party and the techniques through which this responsibility is implemented are not, as yet, rationalized in formal institutional terms.

In a democratic society, decision-making appears to be either in the hands of the people—through their amending or constituent power—or in the hands of their representatives nominated through an open electoral system. Political parties are instruments that mold public opinion, but they rely upon persuasion rather than upon monopolistic control of the media of communication. There is competition for a vote and, as a result, policies reflect as much of a variety of interests as possible. This, in turn, means that a democratic party tends to be inclusive rather than exclusive. Political leadership has to meet the test of popular criticism and scrutiny and its claims to power are commensurate with its ability to persuade. Finally, responsibility is established through rationalized patterns known by everybody, the most significant being the electoral process through which those who control the organs of government can be held accountable for their actions at set intervals of time. Other procedures through which responsibility is enforced depend on the relations between various organs of government and on the legal institutions of a given system. In all cases, no particular group of persons and no particular interests can retain a monopoly of power or perpetuate itself in power.

The same criteria we have suggested can be used for the purpose of differentiating between military dictatorships, aristocratic systems, tribal systems where formal decision-making and deliberation is at a minimum, direct democracies, and monarchies. In all cases, however, the significant task for the investigator is to establish the proper categories and show their utility by indicating that they can be used for the ordering of empirical reality and the identification of social units to be studied.

THE POSITION OF THE INDIVIDUAL   There is a direct relationship between the position an individual holds in a system and the form of political organization. His status and his role are determined by the value pattern of the system which, in turn, determines the organization of the political institutions. In a democratic society, for instance, status is highly fluid and the roles the individual performs are based upon individual achievement. As a result, there is a high mobility in the system, with individuals being given freedom to change roles and status. This presupposes a responsible government which guarantees the values of individual freedom and makes certain that no individual is discriminated against. The goal is not the efficiency of the state or any purpose of the state, but rather the development of the individual. In this sense, it should also be pointed out that the expression "dignity of man" takes a meaning which, though based upon nondemonstrable premises, can be cast into operationally meaningful terms by indicating the various institutions and social units that implement the basic premise. In a democratic system, the individual is given opportunity for education and the acquisition of skills; his physical and intellectual integrity is protected by a system of law which treats all on a footing of equality; and, finally, he is free to take issue with policies formulated by the persons wielding political power and to attempt to bring about a change of policy and, if need be, a change of the personnel of the government itself. The value system and the institutions that implement a democratic society do not involve a transcendental or community ethic to which the individual is subordinated.

In authoritarian systems, on the other hand, the position of the individual differs fundamentally. He is an instrumentality for the realization of transcendental or community values. Such values have precedence over the development of his personality, his freedom of movement, and his freedom of choice. The responsibility of the governors to the governed is determined in terms of institutional structures which give to the political leadership the monopoly of implementing and interpreting the values postulated. In all cases, we shall find institutional arrangements establishing inequalities, limiting freedom, and restricting the recruitment of political leadership.

In despotic governments, military dictatorships, or aristocracies, we shall again find legal inequalities among individuals, lack of established channels through which the wielders of political power can be held accountable to the bulk of the community, institutional and social impediments to the acquisition of skills and knowledge, and legal limitations on the individual's choice of political or personal goals.

In a number of systems, we shall find that the individual's position is regulated by a network of relationships which fixes his status and occupation and which, as a result, establishes social, economic, and political inequalities without reference to ability, worth, or effort. By the same token, custom or the legal order establishes institutional forms which give the exclusive right to political power and decision-making to certain groups of individuals because of birth or other qualifications and relegates the bulk of the members of the community to a position in which they have no choice but to be ruled.

CHAPTER NINE

Advantages of the Analytic Scheme

The general scheme of analysis suggested here for the purpose of illustration simply indicates some of the relevant categories under which a host of social and economic and political phenomena can be classified and eventually interrelated. Interrelationships, however, can be made hypothetically in the light of certain basic theoretical propositions, some of which have already been indicated in the early part of this discussion. In each case, the hypothetical statement formulated will have to be studied with reference to a number of political systems for the purpose of tentative verification.

But even more significant is the use of such a scheme for the study of either individual political systems or the comparative study of certain problems. The study of a political system on the basis of the categories suggested will make possible comparison with other systems on the basis of the same categories. In this sense, institutional arrangement and ideology will become comparable. It is irrelevant, indeed, whether we study an African community, a recently liberated colonial country, or a Western system where political institutions have crystallized into well-established and recognized forms. A common scheme of analysis will illuminate at least tentatively common aspects of the political processes in various systems and will suggest comparisons.

Once the scheme has been applied to various systems and the task of description of the most significant institutional component elements and the functions they perform has been accomplished, then we can proceed to examine the same institutional structures in the light of whatever question or problem we have. Some problems will indeed emphasize new areas of study and analysis; others will lead us to reconsider some of the functions we had imputed to certain institutions. We may, for instance, discover that a legislative assembly may be a channel of information for the executive or that it may be a tool through which consensus among the members of the community is maintained or that it is a part of the decision-making process. In fact, in a number of instances, we may discover that the function we took for granted, i.e., legislation, is only incidental to the other functions that it may perform.

The very formulations of problems suggest relationships and point to the study of the operation of particular institutions. Some of the problems that need urgently comparative study are the problems of political change, the nature and characteristics of revolution, the institutions of authoritarian systems, the nature and characteristics of political leadership and its relationship to other forms of leadership, the relationship between technology and political forms and institutions, the phenomenon of the diffusion of ideologies and the impact of alien ideologies upon particular systems, the relationship between industrialization and the growth of bureaucracy, the relationship between specific groups such as labor or the church and the political process, the relationship between the growth of literacy and the performance of the political system, the study of political ideology as an instrument of control.

Naturally problems can be suggested in narrower terms for specific areas. In fact, the concept of area, as we have pointed out, is helpful only to the extent to which it implies an *analytical* scheme with specific applicability to a particular *geographic* area. In the light of this analytic scheme which defines certain common elements that correspond to empirical uniformities, comparison of variables can take place. In this sense, the area approach, if well used, is for the political scientist an excellent instrument for the testing of manageable hypotheses and theories.

But comparative analysis has another very important function to play with reference to the study of institutional structures through which values are realizeable or with reference to an attempt to get a rough estimate of the consequences that a particular action might bring about. First, comparative analysis is the best tool we have for the purpose of supporting or debunking either moral or common-sense generalizations. It can be shown, for instance, that discrimination on the basis of race leads to tension and political instability or that it is incompatible with the operation of a democratic society. It can easily be shown again on the basis of comparative study that sharp inequalities of wealth create an unstable situation which, under certain conditions, may lead to revolution. Comparative study might cast some doubt on the generally held notion that control of the means of communication by a political leadership creates strong discipline and loyalty on the part of the bulk of the community.

Second, comparative study might give us better knowledge of the particular instruments that can be used for the achievement of certain broad goals on which there is agreement. To take, for example, one illustration with reference to foreign policy: the study of the foreign policy pursued by Great Britain in the course of the nineteenth century may indicate techniques through which the security of the nation was preserved on the basis of which certain generalized propositions may be made. Comparative study may also point to institutional techniques for attaining desired goals at the least possible cost. The study of nationalized industries in various countries, of mixed corporations, of the civil service, of health services may provide political scientists with adequate knowledge for policy suggestions based on the knowledge that specific institutional changes will bring about certain anticipated consequences.

Third, comparative study can indicate areas in which certain types of contemplated action may bring about unanticipated consequences. For instance, careful comparative study of underdeveloped areas receiving economic aid might well indicate that a rapid rate of technological aid may bring about political instability that could be channeled into revolutionary political movements. It may indicate that rapid economic growth in a number of areas is incompatible with democratic forms.

In a more narrow sense, comparative study can help us to foresee the consequences of certain institutional reforms. The inclusion, for instance, of minute provisions in a constitutional charter has often an effect diametrically opposed to the purpose of its framers and may bring about a situation in which the constitution is either by-passed or so frequently modified as to depreciate its value as a written instrument through which basic agreement is articulated. The introduction of a harsh penal code is incompatible with the jury system—for comparative study tends to show that the jury will tend to disregard the law rather than impose harsh sentences. There are literally hundreds of such generalizations that can be made on the basis of comparative analysis. An accumulation of many empirical studies undertaken in the light of hypotheses will increase the validity of our generalizations and provide us with the type of knowledge that we can call cumulative—that is, the type that is slowly built upon propositions that are generally accepted to be true on the basis of empirical evidence.

PART III

CONCLUSION

CHAPTER TEN

Implications for Research and Teaching

Goals

Considerable discussion has been devoted recently to the techniques of teaching comparative government, and although the level of instruction differs between the undergraduate and the graduate levels, the over-all goals are, generally speaking, the same:[1]

PRACTICAL The student of political science must develop knowledge of foreign structures and systems. Knowledge of the operation of foreign systems is (a) a part in what is very often referred to as "training for citizenship" and (b) a beginning of specialized work in preparation for government service.

INTELLECTUAL Study of foreign systems plays an important role in the critical analysis of the institutions of the student's country. The very realization of differences brings about a constructive and critical examination of one's own political system. It makes the student think rather than take things for granted. It opens up new horizons which tend to undermine the self-centeredness that high-school education often imparts.

ACADEMIC Study of various political systems is, as has been pointed out, the best laboratory that the social sciences have at their disposal for the testing of generalizations and ultimately for the development of a body of knowledge. At this level we attempt to relate various phenomena within a systematic explanatory frame, to develop hypotheses and to test them. This can be done only at the graduate and possibly the doctoral level and presupposes a thorough knowledge of the political institutions of the various countries.

Techniques

Having made these general remarks, however, about the goals of the instruction of comparative politics, we are still confronted with the problem of the particular technique to be used. Here there can be no room for a one-sided approach nor can we have any definite opinions as to what is the "best" approach.

THE INTENSIVE OR COUNTRY-BY-COUNTRY APPROACH   Such an approach calls for the intensive study of one or two or at the most a very limited number of foreign systems. Our purpose here is to familiarize the student in as much detail as possible with the institutions of a few systems. The student will have to go over the historical development of the institutions, undertake a thorough descriptive account of their structure and operation, and attempt to relate them to the ideological and social factors of the system. Comparison, as such, is only incidental in this case and is used for purposes of illustration or as a device for highlighting particular institutional functions. For instance, it is always useful in describing the parliamentary systems in France and England to insist on the role of the power of dissolution and the organization of the political parties.

A course involving the intensive study of the political institutions of a limited number of countries has some obvious advantages. It makes the student work through a maze of formal institutional structures and suggests to him areas of comparison that he may undertake later on. It makes him appreciate the fact that institutional structures are often embedded in the past and that they often reflect the peculiarities of the particular country that appear to be unamenable to comparison. Such an appreciation makes the student become extremely cautious in making comparisons and helps him realize that no comparison can ever do justice to the multiple and complex factors of an individual country and that it always involves a level of abstraction which can never approximate the concrete reality. Furthermore, the student who has gone carefully through the institutions of a limited number of countries develops a flavor for detailed descriptive work and analysis which often eludes him when he covers a great variety of systems in an "omnibus" course in which the most disparate cultures and systems are presented to him in a panoramic way.

THE INTENSIVE FUNCTIONAL APPROACH   Another approach to comparative study is the intensive comparative treatment of particular institutions or clusters of institutions. We may, for instance, undertake a comparative study of nationalized industries, of the organization and function of the executive and the legislature, of the legal system of various countries. Here we give the student a segment of the political process in a number of countries and after describing it meticulously we point out the similarities and the differences and attempt to trace these similarities and differences to various political factors or to the contextual elements of politics.

The advantage of such an approach is that it trains the student to isolate some institutions or processes that are vaguely similar or analogous and then, after a rigorous descriptive analysis, to attempt to indicate the nature of the similarity with reference to causal factors or to their operation. This, in itself, requires a more advanced stage of empirical inquiry, and its obvious drawback is that the political system is truncated in a sense and that a particular institution is wrenched from its institutional and social setting. For this reason, the functional approach should be preceded by the country-by-country approach which gives to the student a good grasp of the interrelationship of political institutions. Furthermore, it should be used for systems that have a degree of homogeneity. It is far easier, for instance, to use the functional approach with reference to Western European countries or Latin American countries than for the purpose of broad intercultural comparisons. It is one thing to study political parties in Western Europe for the purpose of comparing their structures and functions and another to study political parties in Western Europe, the Soviet Union, and Latin America. Given the great disparity between the configuration of these systems the student who undertakes their study for the purpose of comparing political parties will have to satisfy himself with very abstract categories that will illuminate differences and similarities of a very general character.

THE PROBLEM APPROACH The formulation of a problem prior to the study of certain institutions and structures has the great merit of stimulating the inquiring mind. Indeed, the teacher who is able to present a number of problems or questions to the student before undertaking the descriptive analysis of institutional arrangement has often done the most important thing from a pedagogic point of view. He has given life and meaning to political institutions and, by so doing, has shown their relevance. As a pedagogic technique, such questions as "How do British institutions provide for responsible government?" immediately raise the problem of responsibility as a vital element of democratic society and leads to the examination of the techniques through which it can be implemented.

But the problem approach is more than a pedagogic technique. As we have pointed out, it is in itself an integral part of the comparative method. A problem inevitably presents us with a situation that can be understood only by relating a number of variables. For instance, take the problem of revolution as a subject of comparative study. It is associated with certain characteristics that can be described, and, second, with certain factors that can be interrelated for the purpose of explanation. A comparative study of France and England, let us say, in the nineteenth century with reference to "peaceful change" and "revolution" leads the student to the exploration of questions that would never have been presented by the country-by-country approach.

The problem approach has a place in both the undergraduate and graduate curriculum. In the first case, its proper function is to stimulate the student in exploring some of the most important problems that our world faces today. In the second case, its function is to indicate important areas in which comparative study will provide us with knowledge.

A SYSTEMATIC APPROACH There is no incompatibility between the analytical scheme suggested here and the three teaching approaches just outlined. In fact, all three approaches can take place in the context of the analytical scheme—to the extent, at least, to which the scheme is logically consistent and comprehensive. The scheme in itself indicates the most significant areas of relevance to which the student will have to refer either in the country-by-country approach or in the functional approach or in the problem-oriented approach. The categories suggested in this study are landmarks without which we cannot draw an adequate map of a system and cannot understand its operation. They are so vital that there is no problem or process that can be studied and understood without reference to them.

The scheme, in itself, can be used for a purely descriptive purpose or for an analytical purpose and can be related to a theory for the purpose of explaining various political phenomena. This last task is, of course, the most significant one for advanced graduate instruction and calls for the development of theories and hypotheses. As has been pointed out, however, it is too premature to attempt even to suggest a general theory for the study and comparison of political systems. Carefully devised problems for comparative study are probably the best devices for advanced graduate work provided the student organizes his material carefully around the particular problems he examines and attempts to explain particular occurrences in terms of speculative propositions. A more generalized theory may emerge only when a host of similar problems have been carefully examined and when uniformities in political processes have been identified in a number of systems. The problem approach is a modest beginning that may bear fruit in later years.

Footnotes to the Study

INTRODUCTION

1. Carl J. Friedrich: *Constitutional Government and Democracy*, Boston, Ginn and Company, 1941, pp. 593–94.

2. Aristotle: *The Constitution of Athens* and related texts, New York, Hafner Publishing Co., 1950; also Ernest Barker: *The Political Thought of Plato and Aristotle*, New York, G. P. Putnam, 1906.

3. Walter Bagehot: *Physics and Politics*, New York, G. Appleton and Co., 1873.

4. Henry Maine: *Ancient Law*, London, J. Murray, 1891.

5. For a forceful if somewhat exaggerated statement of this position, see David Easton: *The Political System*, New York, Alfred A. Knopf, Inc., 1952.

6. At the same time I fully agree with the excellent review by Barrington Morre, Jr.: "The New Scholasticism and the Study of Politics," *World Politics* 6:122–39 (Oct. 1953). The utility of conceptualization must be shown with reference to empirical work. At no time should the development of concepts at a high level of generalization become an end in itself. I agree also that the study of some of the most important problems of our century is far more significant than the elaboration of theoretical constructs and the insertion of definitional glossae. The political scientist should be concerned not only with predictability but also desirability and should attempt to study the conditions under which socially desired goals can be realized. The examination of such goals in terms of ethical postulates is also the task of the political scientist.

CHAPTER ONE

1. See for instance some of the best texts: James T. Shotwell (ed.): *Governments of Continental Europe*, New York, The Macmillan Co., 1950; Taylor Cole (ed.): *European Political Systems*, New York, Alfred A. Knopf, Inc., 1953; Gwendolen Carter, John Ranney and John Hertz: *Major Foreign Powers*, New York, Harcourt, Brace and Co., 1952; Frederic Ogg and Harold Zink: *Modern Foreign Governments*, New York, The Macmillan Co., 1953.

2. Some of the best illustrations of this approach are David Thomson: *Democracy in France*, New York, Oxford University Press, 1952; A. Soulier: *L'Instabilité Ministerielle*, Paris, Sirey, 1939; François Goguel: *La Politique des Partis sous la Troisiéme République*, Paris, Aux Editions du Seuil, 1946.

3. T. D. Weldon: *The Vocabulary of Politics*, London, Pelican, 1953.

4. Herman Finer: *The Theory and Practice of Modern Government*, New

York, Henry Holt and Co., 1949; Robert Michels: *Political Parties: A Socio-logical Study of the Oligarchic Tendencies of Modern Democracies*, New York, Hearst's International Library Co., 1915.

5. Maurice Duverger: *Les Partis Politiques*, Paris, Colin, 1951; and the excellent review articles of Samuel H. Beer: "Les Partis Politiques," *The Western Political Quarterly* 6:512–17 (Sept. 1953) and Sigmund Neumann: "Toward a Theory of Political Parties," *World Politics* 6:549–63 (July 1954).

6. François Goguel: "Political Instability in France," *Foreign Affairs* 33:111–22 (Oct. 1954).

7. James Bryce: *Modern Democracies*, New York, The Macmillan Co., 1921, Vol. I, p. 4.

8. A. V. Dicey: *The Law of the Constitution*, New York, The Macmillan Co., 1902.

9. Henry Maine: *Popular Government*, London, T. Murray, 1890, and William Lecky: *Democracy and Liberty*, London, Longmans, Green and Co., 1896.

10. Walter Bagehot: *The English Constitution*, London, Oxford University Press, 1936.

11. Dicey, *op. cit.*

12. See John Marriott: *English Political Institutions*, Oxford, The Clarendon Press, 1910, *The Mechanics of the Modern State*, Oxford, The Clarendon Press, 1927, *Second Chambers*, Oxford, The Clarendon Press, 1910; Abbott L. Lowell: *The Government of England*, New York, The Macmillan Co., 1908, *Governments and Parties in Continental Europe*, Boston and New York, Houghton Mifflin and Co., 1897, *Greater European Governments*, Cambridge, Harvard University Press, 1918; Joseph Barthelemy: *Le Role du Puvoir Executif dans les republiques modernes*, Paris, Giard et Briere, 1906, *Le Gouvernment de la France*, Paris, Payot, 1925; Woodrow Wilson: *Congressional Government*, Boston and New York, Houghton Mifflin and Co., 1913, *Constitutional Government in the United States*, New York, Columbia University Press, 1913; Arthur B. Keith: *The British Cabinet System* (2nd ed.), London, Stevens and Sons, Ltd., 1952; Frank Goodnow: *Comparative Administrative Law*, New York and London, G. P. Putnam's Sons, 1893, *Politics and Administration*, New York, The Macmillan Co., 1900; W. A. Robson: *Justice and Administrative Law* (2nd ed.), London, Stevens and Sons, Ltd., 1947; Ivor Jennings: *Cabinet Government*, New York, The Macmillan Co., 1936, *Parliament*, New York, The Macmillan Co., 1940; James Bryce: *Modern Democracies*, New York, The Macmillan Co., 1921.

13. W. C. Bennett: *Area Studies in American Universities*, New York, Social Science Research Council, 1951.

14. Ruth Benedict: *Patterns of Culture*, Boston and New York, Houghton Mifflin and Co., 1934; Melville Herskovits: *Man and His Works*, New York, Alfred A. Knopf, Inc., 1951; Clyde Kluckhohn: *The Mirror for Man*, New York, Whittlesey House, 1949.

15. Some of the most illustrative works are: Theodore Adorno and others: *The Authoritarian Personality*, New York, Harper & Brothers, 1950; Gabriel Almond: *The Appeal of Communism*, Princeton, Princeton University Press, 1954; David Levy: *New Fields of Psychiatry*, New York, W. W. Norton & Company, Inc., 1947. See also the excellent review article by Raymond Bauer: "The Psycho-Cultural Approach to Soviet Studies," *World Politics* 7:119–32 (Oct. 1954).

CHAPTER TWO

1. Pendleton Herring: "On the Study of Government," *American Political Science Review* 47:961 (Dec. 1953).

2. Karl Lowenstein: "Report on the Research Panel on Comparative Government," *American Political Science Review* 38:540–48 (June 1944).

3. "Research in Comparative Politics," *American Political Science Review* 47:641–75 (Sept. 1953), a report prepared jointly by Roy C. Macridis and Richard Cox embodying the deliberations of the Social Science Research Council Interuniversity Research Seminar on Comparative Politics in which the following participated: Samuel H. Beer, Harry Eckstein, George Blanksten, Carl W. Deutch, Richard Cox, Roy C. Macridis, Kenneth Thompson and Robert E. Ward.

4. Morris R. Cohen: *Reason and Law*, Glencoe, Ill., The Free Press, 1950, p. 2.

5. "Research in Comparative Politics," *op. cit.*, pp. 651–52.

CHAPTER THREE

1. For a discussion of the decision-making concept see Richard Snyder, H. W. Bruck, and Burton Sapin: *Decision-Making: An Approach to the Study of International Politics*, Princeton, Princeton University Press, 1954.

2. Earl Latham: "The Group Basis of Politics: Notes for a Theory," *American Political Science Review* 46:382 (June 1952).

3. Harold Lasswell and Daniel Lerner: *The Comparative Study of Elites*, Stanford, Stanford University Press, 1952, p. 1.

4. David Easton: *The Political System*, New York, Alfred A. Knopf, Inc., 1953, p. 268. Chapter 11 contains an excellent discussion of the equilibrium theory and its limitations.

5. I have borrowed the statement from Harry Eckstein's unpublished paper, "Comparative Method: Some Introductory Remarks."

6. Emile Durkheim: *The Division of Labor in Society*, New York, The Macmillan Co., 1933.

7. Particularly Harold Lasswell and David Lerner: *The World Revolution of Our Times*, Stanford, Stanford University Press, 1951, and Harold Lasswell and Daniel Lerner: *The Comparative Study of Elites*, Stanford, Stanford University Press, 1952.

8. The student will find an excellent illustration of such an attempt in Barrington Moore, Jr.: *Terror and Progress—USSR*, Cambridge, Harvard University Press, 1954.

9. Robert K. Merton: *Social Theory and Social Structure*, Glencoe, Ill., The Free Press, 1939, p. 5.

10. Harold Lasswell and Daniel Lerner (eds.): *The Policy Sciences*, Stanford, Stanford University Press, 1951.

CHAPTER FOUR

1. De Tocqueville: *Democracy in America*, New York, Alfred A. Knopf, Inc., 1945.
2. For a discussion of the meaning of "operative ideals" see A. D. Lindsay: *The Modern Democratic State*, London, Oxford University Press, 1947.

CHAPTER FIVE

1. For a somewhat different conception of decision-making, see R. Snyder, H. W. Bruck, and Burton Sapin: *Decision-Making: An Approach to the Study of International Politics*, Princeton, Princeton University Press, 1954, p. 63: "One of the most important methodological assumptions we have made is that only those who are government officials are to be viewed as decision-makers or actors. In other words, no private citizen no matter how powerful, can be a member of the analytical unit *unless* he temporarily holds a federal office."
2. Harold Lasswell and Daniel Lerner: *The Comparative Study of Elites*, Stanford, Stanford University Press, 1952.
3. D. R. Mathews: *The Social Background of Political Decision-Makers*, New York, Random House, Inc., 1954, is a good study of the social composition of political elites.
4. Lasswell and Lerner: *The Comparative Study of Elites*, op. cit.
5. This is the underlying hypothesis about political trends in the Soviet Union following Stalin's death that can be found in W. W. Rostow: *The Dynamics of the Soviet Society*, New York, W. W. Norton and Company, Inc., 1953.

CHAPTER SIX

1. Arthur F. Bentley: *The Process of Government*, Chicago, The University of Chicago Press, 1908; and David Truman: *The Governmental Process*, New York, Alfred A. Knopf, Inc., 1951.
2. The *Elite Studies*, and D. R. Mathews: *The Social Background of Political Decision-Makers* (Random House Studies in Political Science), New York, Random House, Inc., 1954.

CHAPTER SEVEN

1. Alexis de Tocqueville: *Democracy in America*, New York, Alfred A. Knopf, Inc., 1945. Vol. II, p. 12. This corresponds closely to A. D. Lindsay's "operative ideals" to which reference has already been made.
2. Karl Lowenstein: "Political Systems, Ideologies and Institutions: The Problem of Their Circulation," *The Western Political Quarterly* 6:591 (Dec. 1953).
3. On the role of the intellectuals see: Crane Brinton: *Anatomy of Revolu-*

tion, New York, W. W. Norton & Company, Inc., 1938; Karl Manheim: *Ideology and Utopia*, New York, Harcourt Brace and Co., 1946.

4. Lowenstein, *op. cit.*, p. 695.

CHAPTER EIGHT

1. Max Weber: *The Theory of Social and Economic Organization*, New York, Oxford University Press, 1947, pp. 324–92.

2. For an illustration see Edgar Furniss, Jr.: *The Office of the Premier in French Foreign Policy-Making: An Application of the Decision-Making Analysis*, Princeton, Princeton University Press, 1954.

3. Max Weber, *op. cit.*

4. John Maynard: *Russia in Flux*, New York, The Macmillan Co., 1948, p. 177.

5. From Plato on, no political theorist has been able to conceive of a political system based solely upon force. Some of the myths elaborated in *The Republic* perform the function of legitimizing authority. The classic statement on the inadequacy of force is to be found in David Hume's essay "Of the Original Contract."

6. Professor Lasswell's hypothesis does not apply to modern societies with greater force than to some nineteenth-century political systems.

7. By education we understand here the acquisition of skills and the ability to use actively or passively the media of communication.

8. Harold Lasswell and Daniel Lerner: *The Comparative Study of Elites*, Stanford, Stanford University Press, 1952.

CHAPTER TEN

1. See the papers presented at the meeting of the International Political Science Association on Comparative Politics that appeared in *Studii Politicii*, Vol. 3, No. 1 (March–May 1954).